Fourth Grade Readers

Fourth Grade Readers

Units of Study to Help Students Internalize and Apply Strategies

Martha Heller-Winokur

and

Marcia Uretsky

HEINEMANN
Portsmouth, NH

Heinemann
361 Hanover Street
Portsmouth, NH 03801–3912
www.heinemann.com

Offices and agents throughout the world

Library of Congress Cataloging-in-Publication Data
Heller-Winokur, Martha.
Fourth grade readers : units of study to help students internalize and apply strategies / Martha Heller-Winokur and Marcia Uretsky.
p. cm.
Includes bibliographical references.
ISBN 13: 978-0-325-02126-3
ISBN 10: 0-325-02126-0
1. Reading (Elementary)—United States—Curricula. 2. Fourth grade (Education)—United States. I. Uretsky, Marcia. II. Title.
LB1573.H3255 2008
372.4—dc22 2008016459

Editors: Kate Montgomery, Cheryl Kimball, and Alan Huisman
Production: Elizabeth Valway
Cover design: Night & Day Design
Cover photo: Fotosearch Stock Photography and Stock Footage
Composition: House of Equations, Inc.
Manufacturing: Steve Bernier

Printed in the United States of America on acid-free paper
12 11 10 09 08 ML 1 2 3 4 5

To our mothers

Contents

UNIT 2 *Discussion Skills for Developing Thoughtful Readers* 33

Building on the previous unit, this unit uses interactive read-aloud to help fourth graders develop their abilities to listen to, respond to, react to, and think about texts.

UNIT 3 *Genre Study for Developing Sophisticated Nonfiction Readers* 80

Through its focus on biography, this unit links the strategies that have been introduced, taught, and practiced in the two previous units and pushes students to learn how to interact with nonfiction in more sophisticated ways.

In this final unit, students are asked to apply the skills and strategies they've learned about reading, speaking, and thinking to unlock the themes within a single author's body of work and to identify elements of that author's craft.

Foreword

As a literacy consultant, I carry the best of my thinking and practices to teachers around the country, and I carry the best of my tried and true books—the ones from which I continue to learn. After reading this extremely smart book, I will add it to my stack and have it under my arm as one of my essential texts. The authors say it is for fourth-grade teachers, but the strategies included in *Fourth Grade Readers* should be shared with all upper-grade elementary school teachers.

What strikes me from the very first page of *Fourth Grade Readers* is the simple, direct language. Before reading a single chapter, the table of contents welcomes teachers. In our profession, we talk often about books being *teacher friendly* as if teachers need some simplified version of the English language to comprehend, but this book is not *teacher friendly* in that way. This book is *teacher intelligent* and *teacher welcoming*. It is written for the practical, day-to-day in-class use of someone whose job it is to instruct children. It is written for teachers who love books and understand that good reading experiences can produce students who, as Marcia and Martha write, "mature into adults who possess critical and reflective minds."

Simply because of the volume of practical suggestions for units of study and the lessons within, this book will be on desks—not shelves—stuffed with sticky note, notes scribbled in the margins, and references made to the lessons therein. But it's not simply the volume of practical suggestions that makes *Fourth Grade Readers* so helpful. Marcia and Martha know the value of good strong teaching within the workshop structure. In *Fourth Grade Readers* they have combined their many years of teaching, learning, and study into a clear guide for the teaching of reading! *Fourth Grade Readers* is a balance of smart teaching strategies and sheer good sense. To quote the authors, "This is not 'surfboard teaching,' skimming the surface of a topic and moving on to the next. The overall goal is to develop a deep understanding and mastery of the concepts. . . . Knowing that you ask your students to take risks every day should inspire you to do the same. . . . Find your own teaching voice and keep your students at the center of your teaching (251)". This is an under-the-arm, top-of-the desk book to help each teacher find that teaching voice.

—Isoke Titilayo Nia

Acknowledgments

Our work has taken us into many classrooms throughout Massachusetts, Rhode Island, and New Hampshire. The teachers and children we have encountered throughout the past twenty-five years have informed and inspired this book.

We are grateful to our colleagues past and present at the Center for Applied Child Development at Tufts: Director Lynn Schade, who encourages us to challenge ourselves and to think outside the box; Cynthia Smith, a reflective practioner and in-house children's literature guru; Eric Stevens, Shanna Schwartz, Felicia O'Brien, Clare Landrigan, and Tammy Mulligan. Folks from Heinemann have helped us enormously along the way, in particular Kate Montgomery, with whom we shared a cup of coffee and dreamed big dreams that finally came true. Thank you for believing in us and for pushing us to move forward with this project. Thanks to Cheryl Kimball, our editor, who taught us about writing and who always believed in "the book." We thank Alan Huisman, who maintained our voice and brought clarity to our words and ideas.

We wish to thank colleagues who have always challenged us to think deeply, including Education Development Center's Karen Worth, Sally Crissman, Jeff Winokur, and Martha Davis; our consulting colleagues, Tess Hall, Jenny Morrison, Ginny Lockwood, and Mary Ellen Giacobbe; and Robin Burdick, who values process, time, learning, teachers, and children. Thanks to our invisible colleagues who don't even know we exist but who have been silent partners in our work and conversations. We are inspired by your knowledge: Ellin Keene, Susan Zimmerman, Lucy Calkins, Katie Wood Ray, Stephanie Harvey, Anne Goudvis, and Isoke Titilayo Nia.

Special thanks go to all the teachers and students with whom we have worked, in and out of the classroom. Thank you to those fourth-grade teachers who have tried out our units of study with kids and given us feedback. Having a place to try new lessons, talk and laugh with children, and collaborate with colleagues has kept our practice fresh and our stories honest. Thank you for opening the doors to your classrooms now and through the years. Special thanks to Little Harbour School, Dondero Elementary, Broadmeadow Elementary, Prescott School, the Learning Community Charter School, Chickering Elementary, and the Lincoln Eliot School.

—Marcia and Martha

To my husband, Michael, thank you for your support in providing a solid foundation from which I could explore. Without your grounding and encouragement, I would not have been able to pursue my passions. I love you. To my children, Jacob and Laura, you have taken the best and soared in your own lives. And to my literacy partner, Martha, you are the yin to my yang. You push me and allow me to push back. Thank you for asking the difficult questions and keeping the teaching honest. I look forward to more in the years ahead.

—MU

To my good friends and family, all of whom have been steady supporters throughout this process. To Jeff, my husband, who has taught me the most important lessons needed to be a friend and consultant—listen and laugh; meet people where they are; and accept and embrace the ideas they bring to the table. Thank you, Jeff, for always being available and patient, and for talking about work even when you don't want to. To my children: Daniel and Zack, who make me laugh and cry and whom I count on for honest conversation, and Emily, a teacher in her own right, who has been a steady supporter, talker, and a second pair of eyes who never doubted this book would be written. Thank you, Lady Jane, for your ongoing feedback, candor, and conversation. And finally, to Marcia, my friend, colleague, and writing partner, without whom this book would not exist. What a journey!

—MHW

Introduction

Why Focus on Fourth?

It's the first day of school. Parents and their kids hurry through the hallways on their way to classrooms. Outside the classroom doors, empty bulletin boards wait to be covered with student work. As the new fourth graders enter their classroom, they stop to read the morning message, chat with friends, notice book bins labeled with exciting headings: "Judy Blume," "Poetry," "Survival Stories," "Just Good Reads," "Graphic Novels," "Fantasy." Eventually they find a table and take a seat. Excitement is in the air. Their teacher turns a rain stick over, and the tinkling sounds of rice running through the maze of little pins initiates a rolling wave of quiet. The day begins. "Welcome to fourth grade. What an exciting year we are going to have together. I can't wait to get started!"

What Makes Fourth Graders Unique?

At the beginning of the school year, fourth graders are eager and ready to test new waters and chart a new course in their intellectual, social, and emotional development. Paradoxes abound. Fourth graders are eager to please their teachers yet reluctant to reveal what they don't know. They are tentative yet fiercely competitive, particularly when it comes to academic endeavors. They are sensitive yet resilient. Their increasing social self-confidence is accompanied by a heightened susceptibility to peer pressure and the desire to fit in with the group, both in the classroom and on the playground. Nothing is more important to a nine-year-old than fitting in.

Academic pressures mount in fourth grade as well. Parents often feel this is the year in which *real* learning begins. After fourth grade it becomes more difficult to catch up. The achievement gap experienced by struggling readers becomes more significant, since the stigma of working with a specialist is more pronounced.

Fourth graders are asked to tackle increasingly more complex, content-dense texts. Until now, picture books and short chapter books have been the mainstays of their reading life, supportive texts that feature high-frequency words, basic vocabulary, repetitive episodes, and simple story lines about familiar concepts. Fourth-grade texts are less supportive. Stories now have more complex characters in unfamiliar settings and situations. The shift from learning to read to reading to learn gives rise to the *fourth-grade slump*, a term coined by Jean Chall (1983).

To fourth graders, the number of pages, the print size, and the titles of the books they read are often more important than whether they understand them (we call this the Harry Potter complex). We know these kinds of books have inspired many readers and are not suggesting that fourth graders not read them. However, they should enjoy these books at home with their families. In the readers' workshop, fourth graders need a balanced diet of books from a variety of genres. Nonfiction becomes more prominent, and knowing how to tackle it is critical.

Fourth graders are asked to articulate their understanding orally and in writing. They are expected to provide evidence from the text to support their ideas. They need to be able to decode the words, comprehend the ideas, and synthesize and analyze content. They must learn to talk with confidence and insight about what they are reading. They need to learn how to ask questions, make connections, infer, and synthesize information about characters and content before, during, and after reading.

Many students enter fourth grade able to decode words but unable to comprehend their meaning. These students—and their teachers—now face new pressures. The amount of content-area reading increases, which in turn demands that fourth graders use a variety of comprehension strategies to interact with and make meaning of these texts. They must sift and sort through information and determine what's important and what's just interesting. They must read more and for longer periods of time. They must learn unfamiliar specialized vocabulary. They must learn how to be strategic readers.

The Pressure of Teaching Fourth Grade

Just as it's not easy to be a fourth grader, it's not easy to be a fourth-grade teacher (or a teacher at any level) in the current climate of high-stakes testing created by No Child Left Behind and its expectations, which reflect the ideas of people who aren't classroom teachers. The emphasis in teaching reading has shifted from responding to the needs of the individual reader to covering mandated curriculum. In spite of this, we must still teach our students what they need to know to grow as readers from where they are.

In many states, fourth grade is the first year in which standardized tests are administered. These scores are important to parents and principals—and therefore to teachers as well. Teachers feel increasing pressure to have students reading on grade level. Unfortunately, these expectations are not always in sync with what we know about our students' developmental differences and individual strengths and challenges.

Many teachers express concern and frustration with the current state of affairs in education: larger classes; congressionally imposed standards; high-stakes tests; increased curriculum; more students who have social or emotional issues, other special needs, or complicated family situations. Being a teacher is a hard job.

A Focused Road to Literacy

Readers' workshop is a classroom structure for teaching literacy. It is not new and has been described in many different ways (Graves 1991, Atwell 1998, Allen 2000, Calkins 2001, Miller 2002). Its essential elements are exposure to quality literature, explicit instruction in reading strategies and literary elements, targeted small-group instruction, and a lot of time in which children read just-right books independently.

The way a readers' workshop shifts from whole-class instruction to small-group, partner, or individual work and back to whole-group sharing and reflection (see Figure 1) gives teachers the opportunity to differentiate their instruction to meet the needs of their particular students.

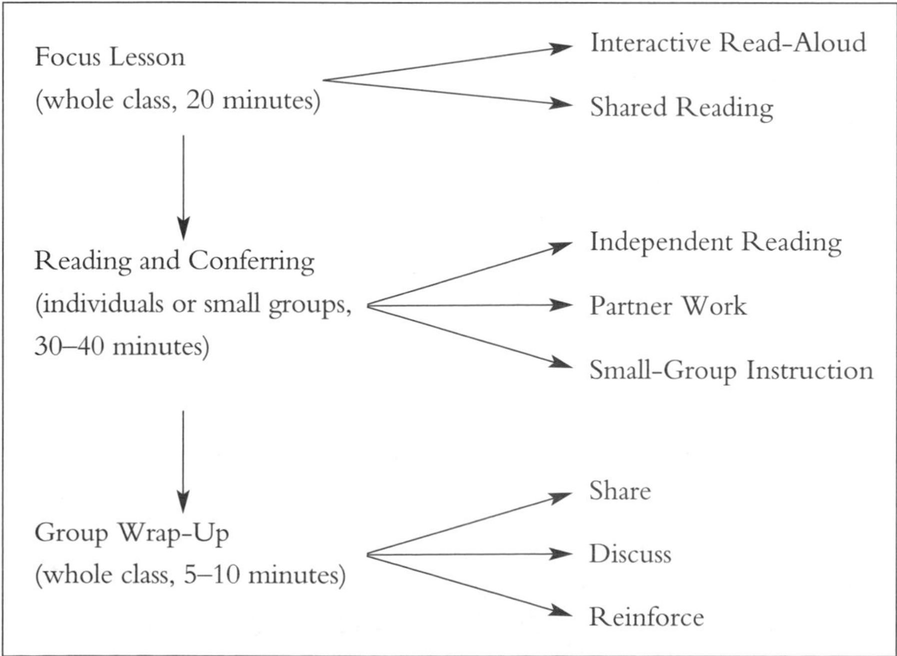

FIGURE 1 Structure of Readers' Workshop

Topic	
Special Notes	
Thinking Behind the Lesson	
Materials	
Connection	
Explicit Instruction	
Guided Practice	
Send-Off	
Whole-Group Share	

FIGURE 2 Focus Lesson Template 1

Readers' workshop begins with a daily focus lesson in which the teacher provides explicit modeling and instruction to students who have gathered as a community of readers and thinkers in a central area of the classroom. This area is often delineated by a rug.

Focus lessons follow one of two templates. The original template was based on the gradual release of responsibility described by Pearson, Dole, Duffy, and Roehler (1992) and refined by Lucy Calkins and the Teachers College Reading and Writing Project. In the more common one (see Figure 2), the teacher explicitly explains and models a reading strategy before the students participate in guided practice. In the second template (see Figure 3), explicit instruction and guided practice are combined as *guided interaction*. This format is useful in guiding discussions and is used primarily in Unit 2, on interactive read-alouds.

Lesson Topic and Materials

Each lesson teaches a literacy strategy or concept, not a specific book. The teacher is free to choose titles appropriate for the classroom, school, or district. Necessary materials for all lessons include an easel and chart paper, a whiteboard, an overhead projector, sticky notes, clipboards (so students have a surface on which to write easily), markers, and so forth.

Topic	
Special Notes	
Thinking Behind the Lesson	
Materials	
Connection	
Guided Interaction	
Send-Off	
Whole-Group Share	

FIGURE 3 Focus Lesson Template 2

Connection

Because new learning is based on prior knowledge, each lesson begins with an explicit link to something students have already learned. Students clearly see that they are developing more complex knowledge and ability.

Explicit Instruction

During this part of the lesson, the teacher, using a chosen text, models a reading strategy and explains an underlying concept. The students listen and watch. After modeling, the teacher may ask, *What did you notice?* This prompts students to articulate their understanding of the strategy or concept before they apply it themselves.

Guided Practice

During this phase, the teacher guides students as they practice the new strategy individually or with a reading partner before they go off to read independently.

Send-Off

The teacher then states any necessary reminders, directions, or expectations, and students (usually independently, occasionally with a partner) apply the strategy or concept while reading just-right books they have selected on their own. As the students read, the teacher confers with individuals, offering differentiated instruction to meet everyone's needs. (Unit 4, "Author

Study for Developing Analytical Readers," includes sample questions you might ask when you are conferring with a student during independent reading. A Blank Conference sheet is included in Appendix B.)

Small-Group Instruction

While students are reading independently, the teacher may gather a small group of students with similar needs for fifteen or twenty minutes of targeted instruction. This needs to be done *in addition to*, not in lieu of, individual conferences. Every student need not be part of a small group, and every small group need not meet every day. One option is to conduct conferences two or three days a week and meet with small groups the other days. A second option is to present the focus lesson, send the students off to read independently, confer with two or three students, work with a small group for fifteen or twenty minutes, and then confer with a couple more students.

Whole-Group Wrap-Up

Every readers' workshop ends with the whole class celebrating, discussing, or reinforcing how students applied the strategy while reading independently.

A Word About Units of Study

Teaching reading today may be very different from how your college education courses recommended it be taught, especially if your college days were quite some time ago. Reading is much more than following a particular story. Teachers must help all students become strategic readers who can internalize and then apply the skills and strategies they have been taught to all the books they read, not just the book they are reading at the moment. Only by modeling and teaching explicitly can we show our students how to do this.

Based on conversations with teachers, administrators, and students, we have come to understand how important it is to have specific focus lessons in hand that address a particular set of learning outcomes. Units of study allow us to teach literacy in an organized way rather than rely on "popcorn"—random, disconnected—lessons. Each unit includes a progression of focus lessons centered on a literacy skill, strategy, or genre that helps empower students as readers, thinkers, speakers, and writers. Each lesson has a specific teaching point, and these teaching points become more sophisticated over time.

This book, which addresses the growing pressures on both fourth-grade students and fourth-grade teachers, includes two strategy units, a genre unit, and an author unit. Being Present in Your Reading: Using Active Reading Strategies launches the year by emphasizing reading with engagement. Building on that engagement, the second unit, Becoming Thoughtful

Readers, Speakers, Thinkers, and Writers, uses interactive read-alouds to help fourth graders develop the ability to listen, respond, react, and think about text with ease. The biography unit links the strategies that have been introduced, taught, and practiced in the previous two units and pushes students to interact with nonfiction in a more sophisticated way. In a final unit, students are asked to apply the skills and strategies they have learned about reading, speaking, and thinking to unlock the themes and big ideas within a single author's body of work and identify elements of that author's craft.

These units in combination ensure that all fourth graders understand the value of talk, internalize and apply the importance of thinking, and continue as active and engaged readers who are not afraid to ask questions and debate ideas.

Each unit begins with an overview of the lessons within it, which you can use as a road map. The sequence has been designed with care, and the lessons have been field-tested with many fourth graders. But, as you well know, students are not cardboard cutouts—each one a duplicate of the previous one. You must revise these lessons and write new ones that meet *your* students' needs as indicated by your conference notes, running records, and other informal reading assessments. To that end, be sure to apply the strategies to shorter rather than longer texts so that students don't lose interest. Ongoing assessment will help you decide whether lessons need to be repeated using alternate texts.

Obviously, you will also need to present these lessons using language and vocabulary that feels natural and comfortable to you. The language we suggest is a scaffold (see Figure 4) that will let you focus on teaching and responding to students in your unique way without worrying about creating each lesson from scratch. Becoming metacognitive about the strategies you use as a strong reader and thinker will help you understand the theory behind the lessons you teach and enable you to sharpen your language.

Finally, your school or district may have different emphases and have schoolwide curricula already in place. The units here can be used as templates for additional units on other strategies, genres, and authors. (For example, the lessons in the biography unit can be recycled and refined and used in a historical fiction unit.) In the final section we provide a framework for designing your own units.

Our work is based on that of Lucy Calkins, Stephanie Harvey, Anne Goudvis, Susan Zimmerman, Kathy Collins, and Ellin Keene, and we hope that you will use their insights as you continue the work we have included here. (If you are designing a unit on reading nonfiction, the strategies in Harvey and Goudvis [2005, 2007] will prove particularly helpful.)

Lesson Topic (Clearly state the strategy being taught in the lesson.)

Special Notes Determine whether the lesson will take more than one class period and note any other special characteristics you want to remember.

Thinking Behind the Lesson Identify the reason for presenting the lesson.

Articulate how and why this lesson is connected to the previous lesson.

Materials Select a text at an appropriate reading level that supports the strategy or concept on which the lesson focuses.

Decide whether you will use a chart or graphic organizer as you present the lesson.

Connection Connect what students already know to what they will learn today: *Yesterday we talked about . . . [We already know . . .] Today we are going to add to that by . . .* Students come to recognize that they are building their literacy day after day and that they are expected to continue to use what they already know. This helps them see skills and knowledge as tools rather than as activities and facts.

Explicit Instruction Name the strategy so it becomes concrete and you are able to talk about it.

Explain the strategy in simple language, a key phrase perhaps, and repeat this language throughout the lesson. For example:

sensory image = movie in your head
inference = something that is probably true

Guided Practice Invite the students to tell how they would use the strategy elsewhere in the text. Ask probing questions to guide their thinking. Reinforce how the strategy is helping them understand the material better and making them stronger readers.

FIGURE 4 Focus Lesson Planning Sheet

Send-Off Remind the students of the purpose of the strategy or concept before they begin reading independently. (They may apply it to unread portions of your example text, other short texts you've chosen, or their own independently chosen books.)

Group Wrap-Up Have students share how they used the strategy by:

Sharing a section of text where you applied the strategy.

Identifying what made using the strategy challenging.

Summarizing and reinforcing.

Getting Started

Assessing and Differentiating Fourth-Grade Readers

The units of study in this book are designed to make the invisible reading, thinking, speaking, and writing processes that strong readers, speakers, and writers use crystal clear and concrete. The focus lessons within the units uncover, name, and model the strategies and moves needed to respond thoughtfully to text. Gerald Duffy's research substantiates "that strategies can be directly taught and that direct teaching of strategies benefits struggling readers" (2002, 33). Richard Allington (1995) teaches us that "there is no quick fix," no magic program, no one trajectory lessons should take. What we do have is research-based best practice: reading strategies applied during extended periods of time spent reading books students can actually read coupled with expert instruction that provides fertile ground in which students can grow. To accomplish this, we need to know who our students are as readers and writers. What combination of reading skills, strategies, and motivations does each new fourth grader bring into the classroom?

Initial Reading Conferences

Readers' workshop should begin right away, with the first few days spent establishing procedures and taking the pulse of the class. Are the students able to direct their energy toward reading books? For how long? Are they sitting in comfortable spaces where they can focus? Are the books they select right for their reading ability? By the second week, you can begin holding reading conferences in order to assess each student as a reader.

Students need to know how to select just-right books that they can read and understand and that they *want* to read. Asking students why and how they selected a text helps you learn whether they have a purpose for their reading. For example,

- Why did you choose this book?
- How do you know it's just-right for you?

They might choose a book because a friend made a recommendation or it's the next book in a series or to learn more about a topic. Then a brief discussion about the text helps you learn whether they are thoughtful readers who can articulate their thinking. Questions to ask include the following:

- What is happening in the book now? How did things get to this point?
- What have you learned about the main character so far?
- Why do you think this character is behaving this way?
- What have you learned while reading this book?
- What is something you have found interesting? Why?

You should also ask students to read a brief passage aloud to check their fluency and ability to decode words. Inquire further about what is happening in the story to see whether students comprehend what they are reading and whether they can summarize clearly what they have read to that point.

During these initial reading conferences, be sure to ask students to tell you about themselves as readers to assess how they view their literary identity:

- Tell me about yourself as a reader.
- What kind of books do you like to read?
- Which genres do you read? Do you read nonfiction?
- Do you have any favorite authors? Series? Characters?
- What goals do you have for yourself as a reader?

The form in Figure 5 is an example of questions that will help you learn about your students as they begin fourth grade. A copy of the form is in Appendix A. You will also find a form for ongoing reading conferences in Appendix B to keep track of information throughout the year.

Assessing Metacognitive Knowledge

When fourth graders encounter difficulty with text, they reveal what they know about using reading strategies to repair their reading. Observing their behavior and asking questions (see Figure 6) helps you tease out what they know about strategic reading.

Initial Reading Conference Form

Student ______________________________ Date ______________

Grade ________________

Teacher Question/Request	Student Response	Resulting Goals for Instruction
What book are you reading?		
How do you select books for independent reading? What do you look for?		
Why did you pick this book?		
What is your favorite type of book to read? Why?		
What is happening in the story?		
Read a bit aloud to me. *While the child is reading, make the following determinations.* *Is it a just-right book?* *List any decoding errors.* *Comment on fluency.* *List evidence of comprehension.* *Can the student discuss the text fluently?* *At a point, stop and ask,* What are you thinking?		
What do you do if you find what you're reading confusing?		
What do you do if you come to a word you don't know?		
What is a goal you have for yourself as a reader?		
Observations:		

FIGURE 5 Initial Reading Conference Form

Student Behavior	Teacher Prompt
Student comes to a word she or he cannot decode.	*What can you do to figure out that word?* *Which strategy could you try?* *What else can you do?*
It is apparent from awkward decoding or lack of comprehension that vocabulary is unfamiliar.	*What do you do when you come to an unfamiliar word?* *Which strategies might you try to figure out what that word means?*
Student does not correct a miscue and therefore does not appear to be monitoring the meaning of what is being read.	If the student has not noticed the miscue by the time the sentence is finished, say: *You read that sentence like this.* [Repeat how student read sentence.] *Does that make sense?* *What do you do when your reading doesn't make sense?* *Do you know when your reading doesn't make sense?* *How do you know?*
Student cannot retell the story or answer questions about it.	*When you are reading, what are you thinking about?* *Which strategies do you use to help you remember what you read?*
Student's retelling of a story or answers to questions about it are incorrect or based on background knowledge.	*Show me in the story where that happened.* *When you are reading, what do you think about?* *How do you hold the story in your head?*

FIGURE 6 Prompts to Assess Metacognitive Knowledge

Reading Inventories

Reading proficiency is a unique combination of strengths and weaknesses. Administering a reading assessment early in the school year will help you determine students' ability to decode, comprehend, and read with fluency. This assessment consists of listening to them read text aloud, asking them to tell what the passage is about, and then asking them questions requiring literal and inferential responses. This information helps you determine a student's instructional reading level. There are a number of reading inventories on the market today; among them are the following:

- Joetta Beaver's *Developmental Reading Assessment 2* (Pearson Learning Group 2007)
- *Rigby PM Ultra Benchmark Kit, K–5* (Harcourt 2007)

- Lauren Leslie and Joanne Caldwell's *Qualitative Reading Inventory IV* (Allyn and Bacon 2005)
- Irene Fountas and Gay Su Pinnell's *Benchmark Assessment System 2, Grades 3–8, Levels L–Z* (Heinemann 2007)
- the benchmark books and running records available at www.readinga-z.com

The advantage of using a published reading inventory is that the texts have been leveled and the comprehension component provided; comparisons can be made to these benchmarks.

Supporting All Learners

Fourth-grade classrooms across the country look and sound different, but a typical one will include the following types of readers:

- students who still have difficulty decoding
- disenfranchised readers with little motivation
- students who can decode all the words but whose comprehension is weak
- students who cannot read fluently
- students who attain grade-level benchmarks and make effective progress on the basis of classroom instruction
- strong readers looking for a challenge

Sound familiar? You bet!

All these types of readers need to be approached differently. Carol Ann Tomlinson (Tomlinson 1995, Tomlinson and Eidson 2003) reminds us that teachers can differentiate instruction by varying the content, the process, or the product (outcome). Readers' workshop allows teachers to differentiate their instruction in all these ways. During the focus lessons all students are offered grade-level content within grade-level text. The content is then differentiated when students select their own books to read independently. The process of instruction is differentiated because readers' workshop allows for flexible groupings (the whole class, small groups, partnerships, and independent work). Teachers provide varying levels of support that allow students to produce oral and written products that reflect their understanding. Following are some specific suggestions for helping all your students develop the reading skills they need to be successful.

Students Who Have Difficulty Decoding

Fourth graders who still have difficulty decoding have often developed coping strategies and behavior to make it through the assignment. Some pretend to have read books they believe are considered cool. Others plow through assigned texts and assume their fuzzy perception of what they've read is normal.

But by fourth grade, reading demands are faster paced and more difficult, and these students can no longer make a pretense of keeping up. An assessment that isolates phonetic elements will clearly show where breakdowns occur. A list of 120 high-frequency words that make up about 50 percent of reading at the fourth-grade level (Nagy and Anderson 1984; see Appendix F) lets you assess whether students know these words and with what degree of automaticity. You can then target specific instruction accordingly.

However, this phonics and vocabulary instruction needs to be *in addition to*, not instead of, readers' workshop (where students learn how to integrate strategies and think like a reader). Phonetic instruction is similar to playing scales on the piano to learn the notes. In readers' workshop students use the notes to create music—that is, meaning. Finding an additional twenty or so minutes for targeted phonics and syllabication instruction is critical for these readers. Focus on the various vowels in one-syllable words and then move on to two-syllable words, teaching students to use the vowels to identify syllabic patterns and break the words into parts. Also teach common affixes to base words.

Disfluent Readers

Naturally, students who have difficulty decoding words will not be fluent readers, especially when the text is very difficult. The most effective strategies to combat slow, awkward phrasing are repeated readings of short, easy text such as poetry (Dowhower 1987; Rasinski 2003; Samuels 1979). Readers' theatre is an especially effective technique, since it doesn't require props or movement: create simple scripts of the dialogue in a short text, assign the roles, and have students read and reread them during independent reading.

Disenfranchised Readers and Those Who Demonstrate Little Understanding

Disenfranchised readers can read but don't. They resist reading independently and complain that reading is "boorrrring." Other readers can say all the words, often fluently and with voice, but cannot retell what they've read or answer any but the most literal questions about the material. For both of these types of readers, reading is saying the words, quickly and passively. They need to be shown how to get inside the text to make it come alive. They need to learn to create mental images, to talk back to the characters and the author.

Interactive read-alouds (see Unit 2) are one way to develop these skills, but remember that students like these hold back during whole-class discussions. Small-group instruction is a more effective approach: there is safety in smaller numbers, and you can set up many opportunities for the students to participate. Asking, *What are you thinking?* shows you expect them to have a reaction, to get involved. Initially, accept anything they say: *That sounds interesting. Tell me more. I'm curious about that.* Then ask, *Who else had that same idea?* to show them they are not alone, that others have these same ideas, that it is safe to share. Later, mold the conversation to sharpen their thinking and help them develop their ideas: *What do you think about the character now? What makes you think that? What evidence are you using?*

These students often require heavy scaffolds during the first few chapters, when the characters are introduced, the setting is established, and the plot is initially revealed. Turning these chapters into a readers' theatre script and acting out the scenes helps them deepen their involvement. Becoming a character in the story, they begin to understand his or her situation. They are forced to be present; reading becomes exciting.

When they reach the middle of the text, they probably have enough of the story under their belts to be able to read a chapter or two independently or with a partner. However, this is also often when students are tempted to abandon a book; keep the small-group discussions going to maintain their active involvement in the story. Constantly assessing their stamina and comprehension helps you know when to rein your students in and when to let them run.

Students with a Limited Vocabulary

The work of Beck, McKeown, and Kucan (2002) highlights trade books as rich sources of vocabulary. Text used in focus lessons exposes students to rich language and literature.

To own a word, we must use it in multiple contexts. During interactive read-aloud discussions, prompt students to articulate their ideas clearly and specifically, to find precise words instead of generic words, such as *good*, *nice*, and *fun*, to describe a character. As they develop theories about what they are reading, students will use key language and vocabulary to explain, characterize, and define their thinking. Talking as a group and reading with a partner encourage the exchange of ideas while developing a more sophisticated vocabulary.

Students Who Are Reading on Grade Level

Students who are reading on grade level are ready to profit from regular fourth-grade classroom instruction, to go beyond the level of reading expected in the primary grades and develop into thoughtful, independent learners. Nevertheless, the more complex curriculum still poses challenges and demands you must help them meet. The units in this book explicitly teach and model the deeper thinking, synthesis, and articulation skills asked of fourth graders.

Students Who Are Ready for a Challenge

Students who have already met grade-level benchmarks are a challenge simply because they too require individual attention. They wholeheartedly participate in read-aloud discussions and need to learn not to dominate them but to invite others to participate and listen to what is being said. Once they learn the language and moves of discussion, they can form a small book club that reads and discusses a more sophisticated text.

Scaffolding Thinking, Speaking, and Writing

If you can say it, you can write it. Scaffolds help students bridge the progression from reading to thinking to speaking to writing. Tools that help students articulate their thinking include appropriate texts, teacher prompts, sentence stems, paragraph frames, talkmarks, sticky notes, thinkmarks, graphic organizers, and partnership work.

Appropriate Texts

Once you know the reading levels of your students, collect a variety of texts that match the range of levels in the class. Texts are everywhere—magazines, anthologies, book chapters—and should also include a range of styles within the genre on which you're focusing. Students need to see the possibilities. Remember, fourth graders' reading stamina varies. Books with pictures will motivate some readers and support their comprehension. Students need to practice new strategies with just-right texts. (For more information on understanding text levels and matching books to readers, see Fountas and Pinnell [1999].)

Teacher Prompts

Show students how to articulate their fragmented ideas as complete sentences:

- *Try saying it like this. . . .*
- *So you are thinking* [restate their idea more clearly]. *Practice saying that to your partner.*
- *You might say it like this . . . or like this. . . . How else might you say it so that it still sounds like you?*

Students often know what they want to say but have difficulty stringing the ideas together into a smooth, articulate sentence. By suggesting the appropriate language, you give them the opportunity and the means by which to revise their oral expression. Encouraging students to practice with a partner lets them rehearse and helps them make the language their own.

Sentence Stems

A sentence stem, whether suggested orally or in writing, is another prompt that lets students articulate their ideas as complete sentences:

- I think the character is the kind of person who is ____ because ____.
- I think the character behaved that way because ____.
- I have a theory about ____. Evidence to support my thinking includes ____.

Paragraph Frames

A paragraph frame provides the skeletal structure of a paragraph to help students organize big ideas with multiple pieces of evidence. It provides a structured template on which students can record their thinking as they gather information. After they have enough appropriate material, you can help them present it in their own voices by asking, *How else could you say that? Who has another way?* Some students need more time to master this skill.

Talkmarks

A *talkmark* is a bookmark containing several possible sentence starters students can use to enter and participate in partnership work and group discussions. A talkmark can also specify language to invite others into a discussion or challenge or extend ideas being discussed. (See Unit 2, Figure 11, on page 54 for an example of a talkmark.)

Sticky Notes, Thinkmarks, and Other Graphic Organizers

Sticky notes are always a handy means for collecting ideas while reading. Sometimes students can use them to jot down textual evidence that supports a line of thinking. Other times, they're just an easy way for students to record their inner conversations and hold on to their thinking.

Thinkmarks provide a number of spaces in which to record ideas over time; they enable students to see patterns in their thinking. Ultimately, thinkmarks can be used to revise or synthesize ideas. Thinkmark templates are included in Appendix J.

Graphic organizers help students organize and hold on to their thinking. Simple two- and three-column charts provide space in which students can collect particular information and record their own thinking about that information. This promotes active reading. Using plain lined paper takes the mystery out of graphic organizers; students can create them on their own, at any time, whenever they need to.

Partnership Work

Reading partnerships allow students to practice articulating their ideas in a safe, supportive environment. Students develop and share ideas with a partner until they sound like an expert and are ready to share them with the whole group.

Fourth Grade Readers

UNIT I

Reading Tools for Developing Active Readers

Students need to learn what it feels like to be present in their reading. In *The Art of Teaching Reading*, Lucy Calkins (2001) refers to this as "reading with a wide-awake mind." Stephanie Harvey and Anne Goudvis (2007) refer to this as "listening to your inner conversation." Students need to understand that it is their responsibility to read actively. Fourth-grade teachers frequently say things like, *My students read, but they are so passive,* or *I think my students enjoy reading, but when I try to get them to share their thinking, they don't have anything to say.* To keep this from happening in your classroom, show your students how to use strategies such as sticky notes, two-column charts, and anchor charts to enhance their reading of short texts you know they'll want to read; for example, "The Golden Ticket," from *Charlie and the Chocolate Factory*, in *It's Great to Be Eight*, by Roald Dahl (2000), and "A Play," from *Childtimes*, by Eloise Greenfield and Lessie Jones Little (1979). (Additional suggestions are listed in Appendix H.)

The focus lessons included in this unit begin with a review of readers' workshop and choosing just-right books and then move on to show students how to use active reading strategies, alone and in combination, to make meaning. They teach students how to

- slow text down
- create images in their minds
- talk back to the characters
- activate background knowledge and make connections
- ask questions
- make inferences
- record thinking in order to develop ideas

- use tools to help monitor thinking
- recognize when meaning breaks down and know what to do about it

When we name a strategy, it becomes tangible. Once students know the strategy exists, they can discuss how it can make them stronger readers and how they can use it as a tool to understand text.

In the early lessons, readers' theatre activities help students delve deeper into the story by getting inside the characters—how they talk, act, and react to other characters. After students have experienced what it feels like to be engaged in a story, they are introduced to texts that will make them angry or encourage them to take a stand. Short novels such as *The Friendship*, by Mildred Taylor (1987), and *Shiloh*, by Phyllis Reynolds Naylor (1991), for example, help students understand how characters and their stories have an emotional effect on us as readers and influence the way we live our lives. (Additional suggestions are listed in Appendix I.)

Using Tools to Read Actively and Capture Ideas

Can you imagine reading an article or a chapter for a course and not being prepared to capture your thinking? Proficient readers wouldn't think of sitting down with a book or an article without a highlighter, a pack of sticky notes, a pen and notepad so that they could call attention to and remember important information. It's inefficient to process information without capturing ideas and reactions along the way. Modeling how you use each of these tools is critical. Students do not automatically know how to record their thinking on a sticky note without explicit instruction. (Janet Angelillo's *Writing About Reading* [2003] is a wonderful resource.)

When we capture our thinking over time, we can look back and use that information as fodder for future writing and as evidence to support our developing theories. In the beginning, as with anything new, the notes students record often skim the surface. For example, a student may make a connection such as *I have a friend just like that.* However, after repeated exposure to, scaffolding in, and explicit instruction in the use of these tools, a student's ability to analyze text, make insightful connections, deepen comprehension, and take risks is greatly increased. Students know when and what to record and they learn how to use the information they have recorded to synthesize their thinking over time.

Throughout this unit of study, the class as a whole uses charts as tools for holding on to ideas, strategies, language, questions, and evidence the students identify and discuss. These charts *anchor* the important thinking and synthesis of the group.

Getting Started

Prior to the first lesson, all students need to select three texts: a fiction chapter book, a picture book, and a nonfiction magazine article. Keep it simple: perhaps write a morning message inviting students to visit the class library and make their choices.

LAUNCHING READERS' WORKSHOP

Lesson 1	Lesson 2	Lesson 3	Lesson 4
Reviewing Readers' Workshop Basics	Selecting Just-Right Books	Determining Reading Preferences	Establishing Reading Partnerships

BEING PRESENT IN YOUR READING: USING ACTIVE READING STRATEGIES

Lesson 5a	Lesson 5b	Lesson 5c	Lesson 6a
Creating Images to Get Inside the Text	Using Background Knowledge to Create Sensory Images	Using Background Knowledge to Make Inferences	Listening to Our Thinking and Talking Back to the Book
Lesson 6b	**Lesson 7**	**Lesson 8**	**Lesson 9**
Noticing the Kinds of Thinking We Do as We Read	Merging Active Reading Strategies	Recognizing When Reading Doesn't Make Sense and Doing Something About It	Decoding Unfamiliar or Difficult Text
Lesson 10			
Holding on to Our Thinking			

FIGURE 7 Unit Trajectory

LESSON 1

Reviewing Readers' Workshop Basics

Special Notes None

Materials An organized and well-stocked classroom library, from which each student should have selected three pieces of text prior to this lesson—a fiction chapter book, a picture book, and a nonfiction magazine article

Diagram: Structure of Readers' Workshop

Thinking Behind the Lesson Establishing rituals and routines in the classroom sets a tone and helps you create a community of learners. Structure and clarity encourage a feeling of safety.

Connection *As we begin a new year together, you have been getting to know one another and our classroom library.*

Explicit Instruction *Every day we will have readers' workshop. During these workshops I will teach you the strategies strong readers use, the ways readers talk, and the ways strong readers behave.*

Today I want to tell you about the three components of readers' workshop.

[Project or display the following diagram to focus students' attention as you define each component.]

Structure of Readers' Workshop

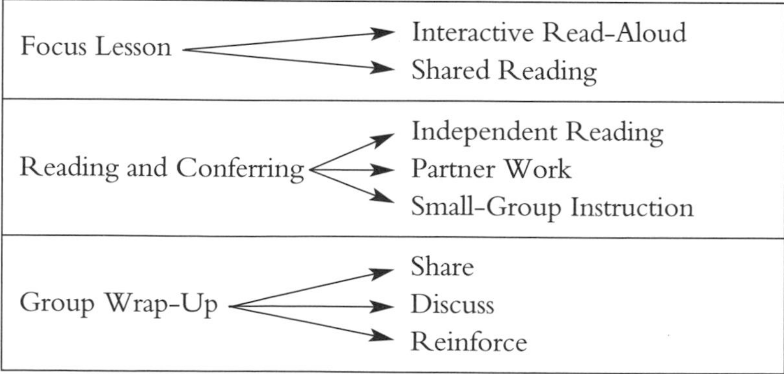

First, we will meet as a whole class for a focus lesson on one of the strategies, or moves, used by strong readers, thinkers, and speakers. You will also have time to practice the strategy.

Then I will send you off to read, on your own, a book that is just right for you.

While you're reading I'll talk with you individually about what you are reading so that I can find out who you are as a reader. This is when I get to work with each of you independently and teach you what you need to know to grow as a reader. Sometimes I'll call a small group together to work with me.

At the end of the workshop, we'll come back together as a group to wrap things up and discuss what we've learned. Often I'll ask a few individuals or partnerships to share.

Guided Practice *Find a partner and explain the three parts of readers' workshop.*

[Monitor what students are saying.]

Send-Off *Today, while you are reading on your own I will be coming around to confer with some of you. I will not get to every person every day, but I will talk to you at least once a week.*

Group Wrap-Up [Lead a discussion about the structure of readers' workshop and how it will operate, but don't talk about specific reading strategies yet.]

LESSON 2

Selecting Just-Right Books

Special Notes None

Thinking Behind the Lesson Reading just-right books ensures that students will grow stronger as readers. In fourth grade, students need to take responsibility for making choices about the books they read and knowing which books will be just right for them.

Materials Anchor chart: Just-Right Books: Easy/Just Right/Challenging

Connection *You have all selected books for independent reading.*

Explicit Instruction *It is important to choose a just-right book to read on your own. Today, I will show you what that means. Look at the three book descriptors written on this chart.* [Point to anchor chart "Just-Right Books."]

An easy book is a book that you can read and understand without much effort. It may be a book you know well and have read or heard read before. It may be a book on a topic that you know a lot about.

A book is just right if you like it, can read the words, and can understand what the author is saying.

A challenging book is a book that is difficult to read and understand. It feels fuzzy. It may contain unfamiliar vocabulary or discuss difficult concepts. It is a book that you do not understand easily and cannot talk about with confidence.

I am going to show you how I check to see whether a book is just right.

First, I look at the illustration on the book's front cover and read the title. Then I read the back cover or jacket flaps to find out whether I'm interested in the topic.

Now I open the book and begin to read the first section of text. Can I read and understand the words? If there are four or five words on the page that I cannot read, it is too difficult. From time to time I pause to see whether I have understood what I have read.

[Model how a reader captures and responds to material she has read.] *If I can read the words and understand the text, it is a just-right book.*

[Model with a second book what it sounds like and feels like when a book is challenging. As you read aloud, make some miscues and wonder about the vocabulary. Give a sketchy retelling; be confused by what you've read.] *I would need to find an easier text about this topic to be able to read and understand it.*

Every reader finds books that are challenging. I know a lot about teaching, so I find most education books easy to read. But some education books are written in very technical language, and they are challenging even for me.

Guided Practice *Take a moment and evaluate one of the texts you selected for independent reading. First review the front and back covers and decide whether the book is interesting. Now open the book and read the first page or two. Put up one finger for each word you cannot read or do not understand. If you find four or five words that you cannot read or understand, then the book will be challenging. Now see whether you can retell what you have read.* [Listen as students determine whether one of the books they've chosen is just right.]

Strong readers know how to select just-right books. They do not pretend that a book is just right. When we pretend read, we are not really reading. The truth is, we are not actually reading until we can say the words and understand what the author is saying.

Strong readers know that everyone finds some books difficult, and that's OK. Strong readers know that books that are challenging today may be just right a little later.

Did anyone decide the book you selected was too challenging? Did anyone find a book that is too easy? [Invite students to share. Celebrate the fact that these students know themselves as readers and were brave to reveal what they discovered.]

Send-Off *Before you begin reading on your own, spend some time deciding whether the three texts you selected are just right for you. If a text is too easy or too challenging, put it to the side and bring it with you to our wrap-up at the end of the period.*

[Take some students through the process in individual conferences.]

Group Wrap-Up [Lead a discussion about students' book choices. Ask one or two students who discovered they had chosen a challenging book to share the process they went through. Tell students who need to switch to other books when they can do so:

- during snack and morning work
- *not* during independent reading]

LESSON 3

Determining Reading Preferences

Special Notes None

Thinking Behind the Lesson Knowing what kinds of reading others enjoy exposes us to different genres and helps create a community of readers who discuss books with and recommend books to one another.

Materials A small collection of books you love

Chart listing the names of all students in the class with space for recording a couple of favorite texts next to each name

Connection *We have been having readers' workshop every day and we have discussed how to select a just-right book. A just-right book is a book that you can read and understand and a book you enjoy.*

Explicit Instruction *We are all individuals, and we all have our own interests and tastes.*

Readers have individual tastes as well. We do not all like to read the same books, nor are we all interested in the same topics.

As a community of readers, we will share our personal tastes in books and authors. This allows us to find other readers who have tastes similar to ours, people we can recommend books to and have discussions about a particular book with.

I have brought in some of my favorite books. I don't select just anything to read. [Share four or five of your favorite books (nonfiction and fiction); include one you are currently reading.]

[Book title] is one of my favorite books. I have read this book several times because it teaches me things that affect me and the way I live my life. Every time I read it, I get something else from it. The way I interpret it has changed as I have grown older.

Another book that I love is [book title]. This is a nonfiction text about teaching reading. It helps me help you become the great readers I know you can be.

[Continue to model the rest of the books you've brought in to share.]

You see that I do not have just one type of book that I read but several different types for different purposes.

Guided Practice *What do you like to read? What are some of your favorite books or kinds of books?* [Give students a few moments to formulate their ideas.]

I have a chart on which I've entered each of your names. Let's go around the circle and each share two or three books that you like. I will record them on the chart so that you can find readers with interests similar to yours. [Record students' responses. Note common and unique responses.]

We see on the chart that three students all love ____ books. You might decide to share books with each other or read the same book and discuss it.

I notice that ____ is the only reader who mentioned books on [specific topic]. Perhaps you can share some of these books with us.

Send-Off *Today, while you are reading on your own, notice the books you have selected. Are any of your classmates reading the same book, another book by that author, or a book from that series?*

When we come back to wrap up the workshop, we will form small groups of readers who have the same interests. Bring a book with you that you want to share.

Group Wrap-Up [Help students find classmates who have common interests in books.

Invite small-group discussions; have students ask one another:

- What did [do] you think about this book? What do you like about it?
- Have you read other books in this series [by this author]?
- Do you plan on reading any other books in this series [by this author]?]

Readers have individual tastes. We can discuss books with and recommend books to other readers who have tastes like ours. Listening to what other people like and why can make us aware of books we are not familiar with and broaden our knowledge and our cultural awareness.

LESSON 4

Establishing Reading Partnerships

Special Notes This lesson should be repeated over a period of several days.

Thinking Behind the Lesson Reading partnerships are a way for students to develop voice. Partners share ideas, clarify confusions, and develop new thinking.

Materials A chart or transparency of a short example text

Anchor chart: Reading Partnerships: What Partners Say and Do

Before the Lesson Predetermine student partnerships (mostly pairs, perhaps some threesomes).

Connection *Our readers' workshop is off and running. We have discussed just-right books and we have begun to share our individual preferences. You have had the opportunity to discuss your reading preferences with your classmates.*

Explicit Instruction *Today, I am going to assign you a reading partner with whom you'll talk about books and share your ideas. Talking with your reading partner lets you practice sharing and developing your ideas. It's sort of like trying a new move over and over during soccer practice. Your partner can ask you questions to help you clarify what you are saying. Your partner may also share an idea that hasn't occurred to you yet.*

As I assign reading partners, move next to each other in the circle. I picked partners who I feel will be a good match based on what I know about you as readers. You will have the same reading partners for a while so that you can learn about each other as readers and speakers. It takes time to develop a partnership. As partners get to know and become comfortable with each other, talk becomes easier and deeper. Partners learn to push back at each other's thinking in polite ways that help them refine their ideas. [Announce the partnerships and have them sit together.]

I have asked ____ to be my reading partner to show you how partnerships work. Today I have selected a short text titled ____. I will begin to read aloud and when I reach a spot I want to talk about, I'll share my thinking with my partner and find out her reaction. Your job is to observe what we say and do as partners.

[Read the first section of text aloud and stop at an appropriate spot. Turn to your reading partner and share your thinking.] *I think what is meant here is that _____. What do you think?*

[Address the class.] *Do you see how my partner and I turn to face each other? First one of us speaks and the other listens. Then we switch. When we talk with our partners, we listen, share, ask questions, and respond.*

[Read a bit more of the text and stop at a second point. Turn to your partner.] *What do you think about that?* [Model active listening by looking your partner in the eye and leaning in to listen.]

What makes you think that? [Model sharing your thinking about what your partner says.] *I had a different [the same] idea because . . .*

[Address the class.] *What were my partner and I saying and doing?* [Invite student observations. Record the behavior students notice on a class chart.]

Reading Partnerships: What Partners Say and Do

• Take turns talking
• Turn to face each other
• Nod their heads to show that they are listening
• Ask questions (What do you mean?)
• Agree or share a different opinion

Guided Practice *I am going to read the rest of this piece aloud while you read along with me silently. At certain points I'll stop and ask you to turn to your partner and share your thinking.*

[Read next section of text aloud and stop at an appropriate spot that invites discussion.] *Turn to face your partner and look at him or her so that your partner knows you are listening. Remember, you're going to listen, share, ask questions, and respond. You might start like this: "What do you think about . . . ?" Or "Do you want to share first or shall I?"*

[Listen as partners talk. Prompt students as necessary.]

- *Turn to face your partner.*
- *Show your partner you are listening by looking him [her] in the eye.*
- *Ask clarifying questions (Can you tell me more about that?).*
- *Respond to what your partner has said (I agree [disagree] because _____.).*

[Repeat until the entire text has been read. (This may take two or three lessons.) Invite discussion about what students noticed they did in partnerships. Add these ideas to the class chart.]

Send-Off

While you're reading on your own today, find something you want to share with your partner when we wrap up the workshop.

Group Wrap-Up

OK, it's time to wrap things up. Bring a book or article you are reading with you and share something in it with your partner. Find a spot where you can sit together. [You may want to assign permanent spots.]

Tell your partner why you selected this text; what you like about it, the author, or the series; and why you find it interesting. After hearing what your partner has to share, ask one or two questions to help you find out more information or clarify something that was confusing.

[Listen as partners share. Prompt students to ask questions and respond to what their partner says.]

Now that you and your partner have had another discussion, does anyone have anything to add to our class chart?

LESSON 5A

Creating Images to Get Inside the Text

Special Notes This lesson may take two periods to complete.

Thinking Behind the Lesson Students need to learn to be flexible with the strategies they have learned. When you create images as a reader, you are using all of your senses and therefore are able to be present and engaged in your reading.

Materials A chart or transparency of a short example text

A copy of the example text for each student

Connection *We've been having readers' workshop every day, and we have set up reading partnerships to help us share and discuss our reading.*

Explicit Instruction *Today, I want to talk about what it means to be present in your reading. When you are present in school you are physically here. Being present in your reading means you are thinking about the story, the characters, and what is happening to them. You are not thinking about recess or playing soccer after school. Your mind is focused and present in your reading.*

Readers use strategies to be present in their reading. One strategy readers use is to create images in their minds—mind movies—about what they are reading. When we create sensory images, we use our senses to see, hear, feel, smell, and even taste what is happening in the text.

Sensory images allow readers to enter the setting where the story is taking place, to stand next to the characters and hear their voices, see their expressions, and feel their emotions. Sometimes our images are so strong that we completely enter the story and forget where we are and what time it is.

I'm going to read a piece titled _____ and share the images my mind is creating. I am going to focus my mind on the text by listening closely to the words the author has written. I am not thinking about lunch or the errands I need to do after school. I am focused on the words in the text so that I can create an image in my mind. [Begin to read the piece aloud and stop when you've collected enough information to be able to create an image.]

- *When I read this part here* [underline or box words on chart or transparency], *I can just see the character. He is . . .*
- *I can see that scene happening in my mind.*

- *I can see the setting where the story is taking place. It looks like . . .*
- *I can hear the character talking. He is saying it like this . . .*

[Read two or three more portions of text and describe the image the words create in your head by thinking aloud and explaining the details.]

Do you see how I use the words the author wrote to help form an image in my mind? This helps me focus my attention on the text and be present in my reading.

Guided Practice *Follow along as I read the next section of text aloud. Use the words in the text to create sensory images.* [Read the next section of text aloud and stop when enough information has been conveyed for students to be able to create an image.] *Can you see that happening? What images do you see in your mind?* [Invite a student to share. Prompt the student to share increasingly vivid details.]

- *What does the character look like?*
- *What color hair does the character have in your image? Is she tall or short, thin or heavy?*
- *What does the character's voice sound like? How do you think the character said that? What did his expression look like?*
- *Show me what the character did. Move your body that way.*

[Invite other students to share their images.]

Different readers create different images. The ones I create depend on my background knowledge. If a character reminds me of someone I know, my image of the character will look like that person. If I have visited a place like the one in the book, I will use that memory to inform my image.

[Continue reading the rest of the example text and having the students create images. This may take an additional period.]

Send-Off *Today, when you are reading on your own, be present in your reading and enter the text by creating images in your mind. When I confer with you, I will ask you to share the images you have created.*

Group Wrap-Up [Select one or two students to read a short piece of text and share the images they created in their mind to help them enter the text.]

LESSON 5B

Using Background Knowledge to Create Sensory Images

Special Notes This lesson should be repeated over a period of several days.

Thinking Behind the Lesson Using what we know to create sensory images encourages us to make personal connections to the text. Comprehending what we read is easier if we can connect and relate what we already know to what we have read.

Materials A chart or transparency of a short example text

A copy of the example text for each student

Connection *We have been practicing creating sensory images so that we can enter the text and be present in our reading.*

Explicit Instruction *Today, I am going to show you how I use my background knowledge and personal experiences to create images that help me understand what is happening in the text. Connecting my background knowledge to what is happening in the text is an active reading strategy.*

Our background knowledge consists of everything we already know from living our lives; reading books, magazines, and newspapers; and watching television. Because we all have different lives and experiences, we all have different background knowledge.

Let me show you how I use my background knowledge to help me create sensory images and understand what a character is thinking and feeling. The title of this story is _____. It takes place in [city]. As I read it, I'll think about what I already know about [city] from my own experiences (my background knowledge). This will help me form a stronger image in my head about what the setting is like.

[Read a bit of the text aloud. Think aloud as you create an image in your mind that is connected to your own background knowledge and experiences.] *I can see the lights and the traffic. I can see all the people walking in a hurry on the sidewalks. I can hear the city noises—cars honking, sirens, music from cafés, all the different languages people are speaking.*

Guided Practice *Now I'm going to read a bit more of the story, and this time I will ask you to think about the connections you are making from your own experience and how they will help you create an image of what is happening in the story.* [Read the next portion of the story aloud, stopping when students have enough information to create an image.] *OK, turn and share the image you have in your mind with your partner. Be sure to include not just what you see but also what you hear, feel, taste, and smell.*

[Listen to what students are saying and prompt them to be specific.]

- *What else do you see?*
- *What do the people look like? How do they move?*
- *What sounds do you hear? What noises are in the background?*
- *What does it smell like? Why? Where are the smells coming from?*
- *What does it feel like?*

[Ask a couple of students to share. Discuss how bringing their own experience into the text helps them create more vivid images.]

- *Have you been to this place before? What did you see there? See how you are using your background knowledge to help you create a stronger image in your head.*
- *Have you met people like this before? What are they like? That's right, you are using your background knowledge of the people you have met to help visualize this character.*

[Continue this process until you've finished reading the example story. This may take two or three days.]

Send-Off *As you read on your own today, remember to be present in your reading. Use your background knowledge of the places you know, the people you have met, and the situations you have experienced to help you create a vivid image.*

Group Wrap-Up [Select one or two students to share the images they created while they were reading independently.]

Today, we discussed how we can use our background knowledge to help us create strong images when we read to help us understand the story.

LESSON 5C

Using Background Knowledge to Make Inferences

Special Notes This lesson may take two or three class periods.

Thinking Behind the Lesson An inference is something that is probably true. Using our background knowledge to help us figure out what is probably true about a character or a situation in a book we are reading is an important strategy. Fourth graders are able to make inferences once we help them see that they make inferences all the time.

Materials A chart or transparency of a previously read short piece

A copy of a new example text for each student

Connection *We know that strong readers are present in their reading and use active reading strategies to enter the text. We have been practicing using the words in the text and our background knowledge to make images in our minds.*

Explicit Instruction *Another active reading strategy strong readers use is making inferences. The author doesn't tell us everything; the author expects us to use our background knowledge to think about other things that are probably true based on what we do know. These are called inferences.*

For example, when we read the piece titled _____, we used what we know about cities to create an image that included things the author didn't explicitly tell us. We inferred that those details were probably true. Readers also make inferences about how characters feel, what characters may be thinking, what a character might do, and how other people will act.

Today, we are going to read a short piece titled _____. First, I'm going to read a bit of the text aloud and show you how I use words in the text and my background knowledge to infer something that is probably true. By using clues from the text and what I know about the situation, I can add information to my sensory image that the author doesn't explicitly tell me.

[Read first section of text aloud and stop at an appropriate place.] *As I read that section, I began to create an image of _____. I could see _____. I could hear _____. I could smell _____.*

The author didn't tell me this exactly, but I know it from my background knowledge. I used my background knowledge to infer what is probably true.

I also thought that the character was feeling ____. The author didn't say this, but I have been in a situation like that and it made me feel that way. So I think the character probably felt that way too. Do you see how I made that inference? I thought the character was probably feeling ____, because that is how I would feel and how I think others would feel.

[Repeat with a second portion of text.]

Guided Practice *Now I want you to try this with me. I'm going to read some more of the text, and I want you to use the words you hear and your background knowledge to make inferences about what the character is thinking or feeling.*

[Read more of the piece aloud and invite a student to share an inference. Prompt him or her to link the inference to background knowledge.]

- *What information from the text did you use to form that image?*
- *What background knowledge from your life helped you form that image? So you inferred that ____ because you have been to a place like this before [experienced something similar].*

[Continue in this way until you've finished reading the example story. This may take two or three days.]

Send-Off *When you read on your own today, remember that strong readers use their background knowledge to help create stronger images. They infer what is probably true based on what they know. Authors don't tell us everything. They expect readers to bring their own lives and experiences to their reading.*

Group Wrap-Up [Ask one or two students whom you've conferred with to share inferences they made using words from the text and their background knowledge.]

LESSON 6A

Listen to Our Thinking and Talking Back to the Book

Special Notes None

Thinking Behind the Lesson Knowing what it feels like to be present in our learning is something we want fourth graders to internalize. Hearing the characters talking, playing a movie in our heads, and talking back to the book while we are reading help us become engaged and present in our reading.

Materials A chart or transparency of a short example text

A copy of the example text for each student

(You will use these same materials in the next lesson.)

Connection *We have been learning to be present in our reading by creating images in our minds and making inferences using our background knowledge.*

Explicit Instruction *Readers listen to their thinking while they read. When I am reading and creating images in my mind, I hear myself reading the words and thinking about what I have read. I hear myself*

- *ask questions and wonder about what is happening*
- *predict what I think might happen*
- *talk back to the characters or the author, perhaps even get angry*
- *make connections to my background knowledge*

Today, we are going to read ____ together. As I read aloud, I'll pause and tell you the conversation I hear in my mind. I'll also jot my thinking on sticky notes to help me remember it.

[Read the first portion of the text aloud. Share your thinking with the class. Model jotting down a few key words to capture your thinking.]

- *Hmmm. I wonder why he said that. I'm going to write* why? *on this sticky note and place it next to that bit of dialogue.*
- *Wow! I can't believe that! I'm going to write that down and put an exclamation point after it.*
- *That is like ____ in the book ____. I read once that . . .*

[Read the next portion of text aloud and continue sharing your inner thinking and jotting ideas down on sticky notes.]

Do you see how I listen to my thinking as I talk back to the book and the author? My inner conversation shows that I am present in my reading.

Guided Practice *I am going to continue to read this piece aloud as you read along in your mind. Listen to your thinking as you talk back to the book. I'll stop after a bit and ask you to share your thinking.* [Read the next portion of text and pause.] *What are you thinking? What do you hear in your mind as you talk back to the book?* [As students share, jot down some of their ideas on sticky notes and place them on their copies of the text.] *So you were thinking ____. I'll write that on this sticky note so that you can hold on to that thinking. Who else can share your thinking?*

Let's continue reading the text. Remember to listen to your thinking. When you listen to your thinking, you are inside the text. You're actively reading. [Stop at an appropriate spot and ask for a volunteer to share her or his thinking.] *So, you were asking the character ____. Here is a sticky note. Write down a few words to hold on to your thinking. You might write . . .*

Who else can share your thinking? Here is a sticky note to jot down a few words to hold on to your thinking. Did anyone else think that same thing? Here are sticky notes for you to record your thinking.

Let's continue reading. This time when we stop, you will share your thinking with your partner. [As students share with their partners, ask them to jot their ideas on sticky notes and place them near the relevant text.]

Send-Off *Today, I want you to finish reading this piece on your own or with your partner. Remember to stop and listen to your thinking to be sure you are reading actively. Jot your thinking on sticky notes so that you will be able to hold on to it. Be prepared to share when we wrap up the workshop.*

Group Wrap-Up *Now that you've had time to finish the story, what are you thinking? What did you think about as you finished reading it?* [Have students share ideas from their sticky notes and invite discussion.] *Hang on to this piece, with your sticky notes attached to it. You'll use it again tomorrow.*

Today, we learned to listen to our thinking as we talked back to the book. When we are aware of our thinking, it means we are present in our reading and using active reading strategies to understand the text.

LESSON 6B

Noticing the Kinds of Thinking We Do as We Read

Special Notes This lesson should be taught over a period of several days.

Thinking Behind the Lesson Thinking while we read is critical. The process must be modeled and named to make students aware of it.

Materials The chart or transparency of the example text used in Lesson 6a

The students' copies of this text with their sticky notes attached

Two-column anchor chart: Kind of Thinking/How This Helps My Reading

Connection *Yesterday we practiced how to listen to the conversation in our minds as we read so that we are sure we are present in our reading.*

Explicit Instruction *Today, I want to concentrate on the different ways we think and the kinds of things we think about. If we know these strategies, we can use them when we need them.*

We're going to go back to the piece we read yesterday, identify the ways we were thinking, and think about how that helped us stay present in our reading. Or did it maybe distract us from our reading? Some thinking takes us away from our reading. When you are no longer present in your reading, your thinking has drifted away.

[Read the text aloud, stopping to reread the sticky notes you wrote.]

- *Here I wrote that I could really see the image in my head. I will call that kind of thinking* creating a sensory image.
- *My note here says, "____ is a crazy name for a character. I wonder how he got it?" I will call that kind of thinking* being curious.

[Record these ideas on the two-column chart.]

Kind of Thinking	How This Helps My Reading
Creating a sensory image	Helps me enter the text and be present
Being curious	Puts me on the lookout for information

[Read next section of text aloud and model analyzing your thinking again.]

Guided Practice *Now we're coming to the part where you began recording your own thinking. I will read the text aloud and you read along silently. We will stop to share the kind of thinking you did and then discuss how this helps you as a reader.*

[Finish reading the text with the students, stopping to analyze the ways they thought and how that thinking helped their reading. If students' thinking does *not* aid understanding or takes them away from the text, mention that all readers sometimes do this. Noticing that some thinking is not helpful is the mark of a strong reader.]

What do you notice about our thinking? What kind of thinking do you notice we used often? Why do you think that is? Do you tend to use one type of thinking more than others?

Send-Off *As you read on your own today, stop and listen to your thinking. Jot down a few notes to hold on to that thinking. When we wrap up the workshop, we'll reflect on what we noticed about our thinking and how it helped us understand our reading.*

Group Wrap-Up *What did you notice about your thinking? Did you tend to use one type of thinking more than another? Please name the kinds of thinking you did and explain how it helped you.*

It is important to know how we think while we read; we use thinking as a tool to help us understand what we read.

LESSON 7

Merging Active Reading Strategies

Special Notes None

Thinking Behind the Lesson Up until now the lessons have relied on one or two strategies. However, proficient readers merge many strategies automatically as they read.

Materials A chart or transparency of a short example text (it should be very engaging, so that students will be very aware of their thinking)

A copy of the example text for each student

Anchor chart: What It Feels Like to Be Present in My Reading

Connection *We have been slowing down our reading to take notice of our thinking as we use active reading strategies.*

Guided Interaction *Today, I want us to lose ourselves in a story titled ____. I selected this story because I find it easy to get caught up in. We will just read and enjoy it, stopping at appropriate spots to share our thinking.*

[Read the story aloud, stopping periodically to comment on and discuss it. React spontaneously; respond enthusiastically to student reactions. Record these reactions to analyze later.]

- *Can't you just see that happening?*
- *Oh, gosh! Can you imagine the look on his face?*
- *I bet he is going to . . .*
- *I wonder what will happen.*

[After the reading, invite discussion.]

- *I noticed that you really seemed to enjoy that story. What did you like about it?*
- *Did you feel like you were present in your reading? Did it seem like you were right there inside the text?*
- *How did the reading feel to you? What did it feel like to be inside the text?*
- *How do you know you were inside the text?*

[Record ideas on chart paper. Prompt students to explain how it felt to be inside the text. You want them to be aware of what active reading and clear comprehension feel like.]

What It Feels Like to Be Present in My Reading

- I felt I was in the room with the characters.
- I forgot I was in the classroom.
- It made me laugh really loudly.
- I could really see what was happening in the story.
- I could hear my thinking was connected to the text.

I recorded the kinds of things we mentioned as we read the text.

- *Someone said, "I bet _____." That's making a prediction.*
- *We all laughed when _____. I asked why you were laughing and Tom said, "I can just see the look on his face. . . ." That's creating an image.*
- *At one point someone said, "I wonder why _____." That's being curious.*

When we are present in our reading and really get inside the text, we are merging all our active reading strategies. We are using strategies automatically and flexibly.

Send-Off *After you read on your own for a bit today, stop and think how it feels. Does it feel like you are present in your reading? Or does your reading feel fuzzy and a bit confusing? If it feels fuzzy, think about why that might be and use strategies to do something about it.*

Group Wrap-Up [Invite students to discuss what it feels like to be present in their reading.]

- *What did you notice about your reading today?*
- *Did any of you feel you were inside your book? What did it feel like?*
- *Did any of you find yourselves sometimes present and then sometimes not? Why might that be?*
- *Did any of you find that you couldn't get inside your book at all? Why do you think that happened? What can you do about it?*

When you are present in your reading, you know what it feels like to enter the text. You know how characters feel, you hear their voices, and you are focused.

LESSON 8

Recognizing When Reading Doesn't Make Sense and Doing Something About It

Special Notes None

Thinking Behind the Lesson We need to comprehend what we are reading; otherwise, why bother? Knowing when our reading doesn't make sense and then doing something about it requires that we stop and pay attention.

Materials Two-column anchor chart: Why Reading Doesn't Make Sense/What I Can Do About It

Connection *We have been discussing the various ways readers think and listen to their thinking to ensure that they are present in their reading.*

Guided Interaction *Sometimes we are reading something and then realize that it doesn't make sense. Our mind says, "What? I don't get it! What happened? That doesn't make any sense!" This happens to all readers, even strong ones.*

The first thing we have to do is notice that we do not understand. It doesn't make any sense to continue to read if we don't understand what is happening in the text. Once we notice our reading doesn't make sense, we can do something about it.

Today, we are going to begin discussing what we can do when we notice our reading is not making sense. On a two-column chart, we will record the strategies we can use to repair meaning.

We know that readers need to read just-right books. A book is just right if we like it, can read the words, and can understand what the author is saying. A book that is too challenging will not make sense. I will put that first on our list.

Why Reading Doesn't Make Sense	What I Can Do About It
Book is too challenging	Switch to another book

Sometimes I don't understand what I'm reading because my mind strays. Has that ever happened to you? Of course it has—it happens to all readers. When we notice we are no longer present in our reading, we can reread the part we read while our mind was somewhere else. I will add that to our chart.

Why Reading Doesn't Make Sense	What I Can Do About It
Book is too challenging	Switch to another book
My mind has drifted away from my reading	First refocus, then reread the part I read while my mind was somewhere else

Are there times when you have noticed that you do not understand the text?

[Invite students to share their ideas and add ideas to the class chart.]

Send-Off

Today, when you are reading on your own, notice when your reading no longer makes sense. Keep track of what you do when you become confused or don't understand something. Write on a sticky note what caused the confusion and what you did about it. We will share our ideas when we wrap up today's workshop.

Group Wrap-Up

[Have several students share what they do when they are reading and don't understand or are confused. Record these ideas on the class chart.]

We need to know when what we are reading doesn't make sense and use strategies to fix it.

Sample Chart

Why Reading Doesn't Make Sense	What I Can (Strategy I Can Use to Repair Understanding) Do About It
Book is too challenging	Switch to another book
My mind has drifted away from my reading	First refocus, then reread the part I read while my mind was somewhere else
Material is unfamiliar or dense	Read more slowly Focus my thinking Stop occasionally and summarize what I know
All of a sudden the text doesn't make sense	Reread that portion of text to see whether I missed something
I don't get it!	Read more slowly Reread that portion of the text Create an image in my mind to help me
I tried different strategies and I still do not understand	Make a note on the page and read on to see whether I can clarify my thinking Consider what I need to know to be able to understand this text: is the content unfamiliar and difficult to understand? If the book is too difficult for me right now, abandon it

LESSON 9

Decoding Unfamiliar or Difficult Text

Special Notes None

Thinking Behind the Lesson Trying different strategies to untangle unfamiliar or difficult text is something that we need to teach explicitly. Students need to consider which strategy might be useful and then give it a try.

Materials A chart or transparency of a piece of challenging or unfamiliar text (perhaps from a textbook)

A copy of the example text for each student

Connection *We have been learning the active strategies strong readers use to be present in their reading. We have also been discussing what we can do when our reading no longer makes sense.* [Refer to the chart the class created during the prior lesson.]

Explicit Instruction *Sometimes we are asked to read material that is challenging. Reading about an unfamiliar topic is challenging because we have no background knowledge to connect to ideas in the text. The information is all new.*

Strong readers use all the reading strategies they know to try to read unfamiliar or difficult texts. This enables them to get the gist—a rough idea of what the author is saying. Let me show you what I mean.

I have selected a piece about ____ that I think is a bit difficult. I will read some of it aloud and show you how I use active reading strategies to unlock the meaning of the text.

[Read the first section of the text aloud.] *That's a lot of information. I know it is about [topic], but I don't know much about that and I do know that my mind is thinking, "I don't know much about this."*

When text is difficult, the first thing I do is notice that I do not understand what I am reading. Then I adjust my reading speed. When text is difficult, I know I need to read slower. Sometimes

I even read out loud. I tell myself that I can focus and use the strategies I know to get the gist—a rough idea of what the text is about.

Now I'm going to reread what I read before, in smaller chunks, and see whether I can create an image in my mind. After I reread, I will try to paraphrase what I have read to see whether I understand and remember it. [Reread the text aloud and share the image you are creating in your mind.]

Guided Practice *Let's read the next section of text together. I will read aloud, and you follow along silently. We will pause after a small section of text and work through it together using active reading strategies.*

[Read next portion of text aloud.] *That's a lot of information. Let's adjust our reading speed and reread bit by bit and try to create an image of what is happening in the text. The first sentence says . . .*

What do you see in your mind? [Invite discussion as students piece together the meaning of the text.]

This part is difficult to envision.

- *We can try to make a connection to our background knowledge. Let's try that.*
- *We can write a note describing our confusion and read on. Let's try that. We may get more information as we continue to read.*
- *We can turn to our partner and paraphrase what we understand so far. Our partner may be able to add information we missed.*

[Continue working through the text with the students. Spend time discussing confusions, trying strategies to repair meaning, and making the decision to read on.]

Can you see how hard we worked to make sense of this challenging text? We know it is not just right for us, but sometimes we have to read difficult material. We still don't understand it completely, but we did get some meaning from it. This is called getting the gist.

We did not simply give up and say, "I can't read this." We focused on being present in our reading and applied active reading strategies to make sense of what we were reading.

Send-Off *Now that we have read through the text once together, I want you to reread it with your partner. Stop after small sections and share what each of you think the text is about. If you are not sure, adjust your reading speed and reread it again, applying active reading strategies to make sense of it. Rereading is an important strategy readers use to make sense of difficult text.*

Group Wrap-Up *Now that you have had the chance to reread the text and apply your strategies, let's talk about which strategies you used to help comprehend this difficult text.* [Invite discussion. Probe into how students figured out difficult portions.]

- *Why do you think that?*
- *What strategies did you use to figure that out?*
- *When you reread the text, was it easier the second time?*

Sometimes in our reading lives we are asked to read challenging material. We don't have to give up; we can use the same active reading strategies we use when we read just-right text. This helps us get the gist of the material, a rough idea of what it is about.

LESSON 10

Holding on to Our Thinking

Special Notes None

Thinking Behind the Lesson Reading the words and not holding on to or manipulating the ideas is not reading. Students need to learn how to hold on to their thinking by recording their ideas.

Materials

A copy of a short story with an intriguing main character for each student

A blank two-column chart

Connection

We have been working hard on active reading strategies and being present in our reading. We are learning that our thinking is a tool we use to understand text. We can purposely think in certain ways when text is challenging or unfamiliar. We have also been using sticky notes and charts to help us call attention to and remember things.

Explicit Instruction

Sticky notes and charts are tools readers use to hold on to their thinking. I almost never read without some sticky notes within my reach so that I can mark parts of the text with my thinking. This helps me listen to my thinking and hold on to my ideas. If I just read without this tool, chances are I will forget some important ideas. I will also not remember which words in the text prompted these ideas. Sticky notes help me record my thinking and important information. This helps me be present in my reading.

Other times I use charts. My charts are usually just blank paper divided into columns. They help me compare and collect information. If I want to compare or collect two things, I use a two-column chart. If I want to compare or collect three things, I use a three-column chart. Pretty logical, right?

There is nothing magical about these tools. They are tools you can make yourself and use anytime. As a reader, you need to decide which tool will work best for you.

If I'm reading a novel and just want to enjoy the story and remember some things that are particularly well said, I'll probably use sticky notes. If I want to keep a record of which strategies I am using and how they help me understand the text, I will use a two-column chart because I am comparing two kinds of information.

Guided Practice *Here is a story called ____. As we read, collect information about the character that helps you create a sensory image. You may use sticky notes to collect the information or you may use a two-column chart. If you use a chart, write words from the text on one side and describe the image they create on the other.*

After reading, have students compare the information they collected using the different tools.

Send-Off *Today, while you are reading on your own, I want you to decide which tool you will use to help you hold on to your thinking. You may use sticky notes, or you may decide to create a chart. On your way to your reading spot, pick up either a small pad of sticky notes or blank lined paper to make a chart. Then give it a try. Until you practice using these tools, you will not be sure which will work just right for you. I'll be coming around to see how you are doing.*

Group Wrap-Up [Have students bring their texts and their tools with them to the wrap-up.]

How many of you decided to use sticky notes as a tool? Why? What kinds of things did you record on your notes? How did this tool help you as a reader?

How many of you decided to make a chart? Why? What kinds of charts did you make? What information did you record? How did this help you as a reader?

[Lead a discussion of how students used these tools and how the tools helped them get inside their reading.]

As we continue to read and learn together this year, I will be showing you other ways to use these tools. For now, just be aware that you can use them in any and all of your reading. Strong readers know they need tools to understand and remember their reading. Always arm yourself with your reading tools before you go off to read so that you are prepared.

UNIT 2

Discussion Skills for Developing Thoughtful Readers

As teachers of fourth graders, we need to establish expectations, teach routines, create reading partnerships, and build a community of learners early in the year. We also need to introduce a culture of thoughtfulness in which students hold each other accountable for their thinking (Calkins 2001). We want fourth graders to develop the dispositions of strong readers and writers so that they will mature into adults who possess critical and reflective minds. We want students to understand their responsibility to be present in their own learning.

The first step is to help them become strong speakers and listeners. All students need time to talk, and fourth graders are no different. Invite them to share ideas with peers, debate theories, ask questions, and wonder about things They need to learn to express themselves well orally before they can do so in writing.

Language arts is often defined as speaking, listening, reading, and writing, but speaking and listening are rarely taught explicitly. This unit does that. The lessons within it use interactive read-alouds to teach the skills of discussion: using body language, listening, developing and exploring ideas, accumulating evidence and using it to support ideas, extending someone else's idea, generating tentative theories, finding just the right words to share your ideas and theories, revising your thinking after acquiring new information, and disagreeing respectfully.

Why Interactive Read-Aloud?

Some educators seem to think children are born knowing the conventions of conversation. But students today no longer experience that once-upon-a-time discussion that occurred around the family dinner table. Many of them interact primarily via a computer screen or the text messaging feature of their cell phone. Time for talk in fourth grade is therefore important and necessary. Interactive read-alouds let fourth graders talk together in a nonthreatening way, initially with a great deal of teacher support, which is reduced as students become more comfortable with and skilled at these discussions.

In an interactive read-aloud, a teacher reads engaging text aloud to stimulate discussion. Students ask questions, share and debate ideas based on evidence, and use that evidence to develop theories about the text being read. The purpose is to support student-to-student talk, encourage students to explore ideas, and help develop speaking skills that will allow them to take part in any discussion. At first, invite students to say anything related to the text. This encourages participation. Later, encourage them to say something related to the idea currently being discussed. Finally, you can ask them to expand their ideas, to say more. With practice, the language you model will become natural both to you and to them. They will own it. For more information about interactive read-alouds, see *Teaching for Comprehending and Fluency* (Fountas and Pinnell 2006); *The Art of Teaching Reading* (Calkins 2001); and *Knee to Knee, Eye to Eye* (Cole 2003).

The Teacher's Role

There is no script for an interactive read-aloud, no one right way to encourage student involvement. Use what you know about your students and the story or article to plan your lesson. When she was a young child, Marcia's mother taught her card games by playing each hand with cards face up on the table; her mum explained why she played each one of her cards and helped Marcia make smart moves when it was her turn. Interactive read-alouds work in much the same way.

Discussions tend to move through a predictable sequence (see Figure 8). Begin by briefly introducing the text and reading the first section aloud, stopping at a spot that invites discussion. Then pose a question.

Open questions (*What are you thinking?*) invite initial ideas and let students know you expect them to be thinking. They tell students you are interested in their thinking. Open questions allow all students to participate; students are not put on the spot—expected to provide specific information. Open questions let students bring their ideas to the table. Quiet students often discover that their thinking is like that of the more vocal students in the class. You can bring this idea home by asking, *How many of you had this same smart thought?* Or you can open the discussion to other points of view: *Who had another idea?* Readers may think differently depending on how they view the situation.

Direct questions (*What are you thinking about such and such?*) are more leading. They usually involve characters, their behavior, and the situations they

Teaching Move	Purpose
Pose a question: *What are you thinking?* (open question) *What do you think about such and such?* (direct question)	To solicit ideas To let students know they are expected to be thinking
Have students turn and tell their partner what they are thinking.	To allow all students to share their thinking To allow students to practice articulating their thinking before sharing their ideas with the class
Listen as partners talk and note the common ideas that surface.	To assess your students' comprehension and get a feel for their reactions
Model oral language: *So you are thinking . . .* *Try saying it like this . . .*	To help students find just the right words To name what they are doing.
Put ideas on the table: *I heard a couple of ideas as I listened to your partnership discussions. One was _____.* *Kathy and Jane, you mentioned that; can you elaborate for us?* *Who can say more about that?*	To introduce common ideas that will spark the conversation To show students that the ideas came from them, that they are smart thinkers who have valuable ideas worth discussing
Prompt discussion while teaching body language and discussion protocols: • *Turn toward the speaker so he or she knows you are really listening.* • *Before we change the topic, let's see if anyone has more to say about this idea. We can do this by asking, "Does anyone else have more to add?"* • *It's important to share other points of view. Who had a different idea?* • *What evidence in the story makes you think that might be true?*	To explicitly teach the body language, conversational moves, and habits of mind related to discussion. Naming these kinds of behavior and strategies makes them concrete. Students are aware they exist, can talk about them, and are able to use them purposefully.
Summarize thinking: *We have a few ideas on the table. Let's review them so that we can hold on to our initial thinking as we continue to read.*	To let everyone catch up to the conversation and synthesize the ideas before reading on
Repeat the process with next section of text: *I will read the next section of text aloud while you follow along silently. Listen for additional information that supports or changes your original ideas.* [Stop at a spot that invites discussion.] *So, now what are you thinking? What do you think about _____?*	To let students know you expect them to continue to shape their ideas To use evidence from the text to support thinking.

FIGURE 8 General Structure of Interactive Read-Alouds

Teaching Move	Purpose
Repeat process to end of text.	
Reflect: • *What did you notice about our discussion today?* • *Did it get at some underlying ideas?* • *Did our ideas branch out like a web?* • *How can we make our discussion even stronger?* • *Name one purposeful discussion move you used today.* • *Name one discussion move you will try tomorrow.*	To help students become aware of the conversational moves and body language their classmates used and their individual strengths and weaknesses To teach them that they are accountable—they are responsible for speaking and listening and moving the discussion along

FIGURE 8 *Continued*

find themselves in: *What kind of person do you think this character is? Why do you think the character handled the situation in that way?*

As ideas begin to surface, you'll scaffold the discussion by modeling smart conversational moves and body language. You'll then conclude each lesson by reflecting on the discussion, identifying the conversational moves that have been used, and telling students they can add these concrete, purposeful strategies to their repertoire of discussion tools and techniques.

Choosing Stopping Points

The ideal interactive read-aloud text invites discussion, provokes thinking, and provides opportunities to view a situation from several perspectives. Your job is to scaffold and facilitate the discussion as children interact. Some pieces can be read and completed in a single session, but often they will require several sessions in order to give students time for independent practice and discussion. Previewing and reading the book several times before the lesson is critical. You need to identify three or four purposeful stopping spots that will provoke discussion.

For example, if you are reading *The Friendship*, by Mildred Taylor (1987), and the discussion will focus on character actions, you'll want to stop at a point in the story where students will have something to say about a character's actions. But be sure you read enough text so that students can gather evidence to support their theories.

Another technique is to stop at a spot you know will have sparked a reaction and ask, *So what are you thinking?*

Supporting and Extending Discussion

During interactive read-alouds, you'll prompt students to share and extend their thinking. These prompts often have a dual purpose. For example, after a student shares an idea, you can ask, *How many of you are thinking the same thing?*

Initiating Questions

- So, what are you thinking?
- What are you thinking about ____?

Probing Questions

- What do you think about ____?
- Why do you think that?
- What evidence do you have?
- What in the text makes you think that?
- Who else was thinking this same thing? Why?

Extending Questions

- Who can say more about ____?
- Who has additional evidence to support this theory?
- Does someone have a different idea to put on the table?

Scaffolding Questions

- Do you agree with ____? Tell everybody. Say it like this: "I agree that ____ because ____."
- Which theory do you agree with, ____ or ____?

FIGURE 9 Four Types of Prompts

This allows all students to participate, if just by raising their hands. It also lets students know they can take risks and share their ideas without fear of being wrong.

There are four types of prompts (see Figure 9): initiating questions (to get things going), probing questions (to request evidence and explanation), extending questions (to solicit additional ideas and other points of view), and scaffolding questions (to help students who have difficulty articulating their ideas).

Including Wait Time

Interactive read-alouds are a way to break the learned behavior of parallel classroom discourse (teacher, student, teacher, student) and model discussion in which students have voice and ownership. We need to wait for students to talk, not immediately fill the silences with *our* words. We need to give students time to process their thinking. Wait time is critical. It gives everyone a couple of moments to think and wonder before speaking and to use the signals that occur naturally in daily conversation, such as making eye contact, nodding, interjecting, and pausing.

Introducing Reading Partnerships

You can encourage everyone's participation by posing a question to the whole group and then asking students to turn and tell their partners what they are thinking. Talking with a partner is an oral rehearsal—a chance for students to practice articulating their thinking before sharing it with the class as a whole. Given the pressure on fourth graders to read fluently and with understanding, it is especially important for struggling readers to work with a partner. It lets them contribute to a conversation immediately.

Moving from Interactive Read-Aloud to Independent Reading to Group Share

After the interactive read-aloud, ask students to apply the strategies to which they've been introduced in their independent reading. As you confer with individuals, ask them to share their theories about the characters or situations in their stories. Prompt students to gather information to support their theories and identify themes in the text: ask them to record their ideas on sticky notes, in the margins, on graphic organizers, or in their reading response notebooks.

Then, during group share, highlight the strategies students have been using and celebrate the work they've done.

The Lessons

The lessons in this unit are based on our experiences in launching student discussions. However, every group of students is different; every discussion is an organic series of responses among the individuals involved, individuals who have unique strengths and experiences. Therefore, we've identified options based on patterns of behavior. You can also use the blank Focus Lesson Planning template in Appendix O to create your own lessons geared to students' specific needs. If your students are already familiar with interactive read-alouds, quickly review the expectations and move immediately into deeper discussions.

LESSON 1	LESSON 2	LESSON 3	LESSON 4
Engaging in Purposeful Discussion	Mapping the Discussion: Parallel versus Cross-Talk	Using Body Signals in a Discussion	Talking Through the Circle
LESSON 5	**LESSON 6**	**LESSON 7**	**LESSON 8**
Accumulating Evidence	Language You Can Use to Connect Ideas During Discussion	Listening Actively	Collecting Evidence: Jotting Thinking on Sticky Notes or in the Margins
LESSON 9	**LESSON 10**	**LESSON 11**	**LESSON 12**
Developing Theories About Characters	Developing Theories About Characters' Behavior	Revising and Developing Thinking: Finding the Right Words	Discussing Themes
LESSON 13	**LESSON 14**	**LESSON 15**	**LESSON 16***
Sharpening Language and Articulating Thinking by Talking with a Partner	Saying It So You Can Write It	Assessing a Discussion	Finding Ways to Disagree Respectfully: Challenging and Debating Ideas
LESSON 17*	**LESSON 18***		
Using Talking Points	Inviting Others into the Discussion		

*Lessons with an asterisk are intended for students who are comfortable with discussion protocols and ready to deal with some of the finer points.

FIGURE 10 Unit Trajectory

LESSON 1

Engaging in Purposeful Discussion

Special Notes None

Lesson should be taught over several days.

Thinking Behind the Lesson Strong speakers use purposeful conversational moves and language. Students can be introduced to purposeful discussion through interactive read-alouds.

Materials One copy of a short, engaging story for each student

A transparency of the story (optional)

Anchor chart: Conversational Moves and Body Language

Connection *I am enjoying conferring with you during independent reading and hearing about your books and learning about you as readers.*

Guided Interaction *Today we are going to begin a unit of study on having purposeful discussions. I am going to teach you the purposeful conversational moves and body language of strong speakers and listeners.*

One of the things I know about powerful people is that they are strong speakers. People listen to them. They have learned moves, or ways to get people to listen to them. They don't just tell what they want to say; they use purposeful conversational moves and body language to engage others in discussion. They are also strong listeners. They know that if you want people to listen to your ideas, you need to listen to theirs.

Readers begin thinking about the book even before they begin reading. When I look at the cover, my mind searches for information about the author, the series, the topic. For example, I have read other books by this author. [Mention another title.] *Do you see that even before I read, I am thinking about the book? Turn and talk to your partner and share what you think about when you look at the cover and what you know about this author or topic.*

[Listen to the partner conversations and note a few of the ideas that surface.] *How many of you had the idea that _____?* [Let students know they have valid ideas.] *Look at all the readers who had similar thinking.* [Indicate that other ideas are valued and expected.] *Did anyone have a different idea?* [Encourage a couple students to share. You want them to say anything—to take a risk and share.]

[Read the first section of text aloud.] *So what are you thinking? Turn and tell your reading partner what you are thinking about.* [Note a few common ideas that surface.] *I heard a couple of ideas as I listened in on your partnership discussions. One was that ____.* [Invite the partnership who had that idea to "say more about that."]

[Use the following prompts to teach conversational moves and body language. Focus on one or two in each lesson and develop students' repertoire over several days.]

- *Everyone turn your body toward [student name] like this so that she can really know you are listening.*
- *Now shift your body toward [student name] as he shares what he has to say.*
- *Make sure you speak loud enough so that everyone can hear your thinking.*
- *Strong readers use evidence to support their ideas. Explain why you think that. What in the book or from your life makes you think that?*
- *Before we change the topic, does anyone else have something to add?*
- *Before you tell us what you are thinking, let [student name] know you listened to what she said. You might say, "I agree with what you said about ____ and another reason is ____."*
- [For students having difficulty expressing themselves:] *So you are thinking ____. You might say it like this: ____. You try it.*

[Summarize ideas.] *We have a few ideas on the table. Hold on to your initial thinking as we continue to read.*

As I read the next section of text aloud, you follow along in your mind. Listen for information that supports or changes your original ideas. [Stop at an appropriate spot.] *So, now what are you thinking? What do you think about ____? Turn and talk to your partner.*

[Invite students to initiate the discussion.] *Who has an idea to begin our discussion?*

[Continue as above for a few more sections of the story.]

Send-Off *I would like you to finish reading this text independently. When you are done, talk quietly with your partner about what you are thinking. When I see that partners have had the opportunity to talk, we will regroup and have a class discussion.*

Group Wrap-Up *I want you to think about the discussion we had today. Think about the conversational moves and body language you began to use. We are going to begin an anchor chart titled "Conversational Moves and Body Language." Who can share a conversational move you used today?* [List students' ideas on the anchor chart.]

Sample Chart

Conversational Moves and Body Language

- Look at the speaker.
- Turn toward the speaker.
- Speak loud enough so that everyone can hear your ideas.
- Lean in if you cannot hear.
- Nod or smile to show you are present and thinking.
- Use evidence to explain your ideas.
- Make sure everyone has said what he or she wants to about the current topic before changing the subject.
- Show the previous speaker you heard what he or she said: "I heard you say ____, and I agree because ____."
- Disagree politely: "I had a different theory about that and here's why. . . ."

LESSON 2

Mapping the Discussion: Parallel versus Cross-Talk

Special Notes None

Thinking Behind the Lesson Students need to interact with one another rather than just with you.

Materials

One copy of a short, engaging short story for each student

A transparency of the story (optional)

An adult volunteer to map the discussion on chart paper

Anchor chart: Conversational Moves and Body Language (from Lesson 1)

Connection

We have been reading stories and practicing purposeful conversational moves and body language to engage in deeper discussions.

Explicit Instruction

Today, I am going to read aloud [story title]. At an appropriate spot we will stop and begin a discussion about the story. I have asked [name] to map our discussion—to plot how our conversation moves from person to person. A strong conversation moves from student to student, not just between the teacher and a student, the teacher and another student, the teacher and yet another student, and so on.

For example: Janna initiated the conversation by saying, "I think the character acted unfairly when. . . ." Michael responded to Janna by saying, "I have a different opinion. I don't agree with you. I think . . . because. . . ." Janna then replied, "but it said in the book. . . . And in my own life I know that. . . ." Jacob then said, "I agree a little bit with both of you. I agree with want Janna said because. . . . But Michael made a good point about. . . ."

Do you see how readers have different perspectives about situations? In a discussion we listen and respond to each person's perspective and use evidence from the text and our own lives to support that thinking.

Guided Interaction

OK, here we go. As you hear my voice, follow along by thinking and creating images in your head. This will help you get inside the story. Be present in your reading by thinking about the ideas the author is sharing.

[Read the first section of text aloud. Stop at a spot that is likely to prompt discussion and pose a question.] *So what are you thinking? Who can start us off?*

[Allow the discussion to flow with little, if any, prompting. When the conversation tapers off, have the person who has been plotting it share the map she or he has created. Discuss the patterns that surface.]

- *What do you notice about the map of our discussion?*
- *What do you notice about the way the discussion is moving?*
- *Is everybody sharing his or her ideas?*
- *Are there people who didn't share at all?*
- *Do some people talk more than others?*
- *Did people talk back and forth, or did everyone just tell his or her idea?*
- *Did the discussion run out of steam?*

[Problem solve.] *What can we do to make our discussion move through the group like a web?* [Add ideas to the "Conversational Moves and Body Language" chart:

- Ask an initiating question: "Why do you think ____?"
- Piggyback on someone else's idea: "I agree with ____ because ____."
- Ask for clarification: "What do you mean? Can you explain what you are thinking?"]

I am going to read the next part of the story aloud as you follow along in your mind. Listen for information that supports or changes your thinking.

[Read aloud and stop at an appropriate spot.] *This time I am going to stay out of the discussion. Remember to use the conversational moves and body language we've been learning about and practicing. [Name] will plot your discussion again.*

[When the discussion tapers off, examine the patterns in the map of the discussion.]

Send-Off

I would like you to finish reading this text on your own. After you read it, talk quietly with your partner about what you are thinking. When I see that partners have had the opportunity to talk, we will have a final discussion as a class.

[Students can read a book of their own choosing if they complete the class story before the end of the period.]

Group Wrap-Up *Before you read on your own, we were discussing _____.*

Now that you have finished the story, I am curious to hear what else you are thinking. [Name] will map our discussion so that we can assess whether it's becoming more interactive. Remember to use the conversational moves and body language we've identified. Who can get us started? [Select one student to spark the discussion. When the discussion tapers off, share the map once again and examine the patterns that emerge. Has the class made progress from the initial discussion to the last discussion?]

Now that we know that our discussions should be through the circle, we'll focus on learning to build strategies that deepen and enrich our thinking.

LESSON 3

Using Body Signals in a Discussion

Special Notes This lesson will probably take two readers' workshops.

Thinking Behind the Lesson Students need to become aware of body language that will allow them to enter a discussion naturally.

Materials One copy of a short, engaging story for each student

A transparency of the story (optional)

Two-column anchor chart: Body Signals/How These Signals Help the Speaker or Listener

Anchor chart: Conversational Moves and Body Language (from Lesson 1)

Connection *We have been talking about how a discussion should move through the circle and be weblike. I've been noticing that you often look at me rather than each other when you are sharing your ideas, like you are talking through me. You are sharing your ideas with the whole class, but your eyes are right on me. Let your eyes scan the class. Let your classmates know you are talking to them. Remember that you are having a discussion with the group; it is not just a discussion with me.*

Guided Interaction *Today, I want to show you how strong communicators use signals to talk to one another during a discussion. When I talk with my family at the dinner table, we do not raise our hands to speak. We have ways of knowing when it is appropriate to talk. We signal with our eyes, nod our heads, or join in at a pause. When two of us start to talk at the same time, one of us knows to wait and listen.*

We are going to play a game to get you to notice discussion signals and practice taking turns speaking without raising your hand and without looking at me and waiting for me to call on you.

[Explain the rules of the game.] *We have twenty-three people in our class including me. We are going to count from one to twenty-three without being assigned a number and without raising our hands. That means that you may say only one number.*

Let's try it. I will start by saying number one. Then another person will say two and another will say three. Remember that you may say a number only once. If more than one person says a number, you must figure out a way—without using your voice—to go on. If we can't decide who should go next, then I'll stop the game and begin from number one again. The game will end when we have counted from one to twenty-three. Let's get started.

[As the students play the game, discussion signals will evolve. When the game has been played through one time, ask the students to do it again. This time ask students to watch and think about what is happening.] *What signals or moves do people make to let you know who wants to talk? Be specific.* [Remind students they should not go in the same order as before.]

What did you notice? How did you figure out when you could say the next number? [Record their observations on a two-column chart.]

Body Signals	How These Signals Help the Speaker or Listener
Head nod	Indicates "I'm done. Your turn."
Hand motion	Indicates "I have something to say."
Wait for pause	
Make eye contact	Indicates either "May I speak?" or "You go ahead," depending.

We have observed body signals in order to become more powerful speakers. Now that we have observed and named these signals, we can purposefully use them ourselves to be more effective communicators.

Send-Off

[On day 2:] *I would like you to read this story with your partner. After you read it, talk quietly to each other about what you are thinking. When I see that partners have had the chance to talk, we will have a discussion as a class.*

Group Wrap-Up

[After partners have read the story and have had an opportunity to share their thinking:] *I am going to begin the discussion by asking, "So what are you thinking?" But then, just like in the numbers game, you will use body signals to keep the discussion moving.*

[Lead the class in reflecting on how the discussion went.] *Were you able to use body signals in your discussion? What went well? What could we work on to improve our discussions?* [Write down the things the class notes on the "Conversational Moves and Body Language" chart.]

LESSON 4

Talking Through the Circle

Special Notes None

Materials One copy of a short, engaging story for each student

A transparency of the story (optional)

Two-column anchor chart: What We Noticed/What We Can Do to Make Our Discussions Stronger

Ball of yarn (about the size of a baseball)

Thinking Behind the Lesson Students need to practice talking with their peers rather than to you.

Connection *We have been talking about how strong discussions are like a web.*

Guided Interaction *Today, I want to illustrate this by making a real web. As I read aloud, listen to my voice and follow along in your mind. We'll stop at an appropriate spot to talk about the story. As we do, we will pass a ball of yarn from speaker to speaker to map the discussion.*

[Read the first section of the story aloud. Stop and initiate discussion.] *So what are you thinking?* [Wait through the silence. Pass the yarn to the student who begins the discussion. Prompt students to pass the yarn.]

[When the discussion tapers off, lead a class discussion of the web that was created.] *Look at the web.*

- *What patterns do you notice?*
- *How did our discussion move from one person to the other?*
- *Was everyone involved?*
- *Did anyone dominate?*
- *Are there instances where the yarn went back and forth between a few people?*

[Help the class name the patterns that emerge. List these observations on a two-column chart.]

What We Noticed	What We Can Do to Make Our Discussions Stronger
• Some people didn't participate.	• Invite people to share.
• Some people talkd a lot.	• Remember to monitor yourself.

Send-Off *I would like you to finish reading this story independently. After you read it, talk quietly to your partner about what you are thinking. When I see that partners have had the chance to talk, we'll have a class discussion.*

Group Wrap-Up *Before you went off to work on your own and with your partner, we were discussing ____. I am curious to hear what you are thinking now that you have finished the story. As we talk, be sure to use conversational moves and body language and to pass the ball of yarn from speaker to speaker. Who can get us started?* [Select one student to spark the discussion.]

[When the discussion tapers off, reflect on the web the students created. Examine the patterns that emerged. Has the class made progress in conducting an equitable discussion?]

Reflect on the discussion and your own role in promoting the discussion. What can you try tomorrow that will help make our discussion deeper?

LESSON 5

Accumulating Evidence

Special Notes None

Thinking Behind the Lesson Students need to recognize that their initial ideas should develop into theories. Readers don't flit from one thought to another; rather, they continue a line of thinking.

Materials One copy of a short, engaging story for each student

A transparency of the story (optional)

Anchor chart: Conversational Moves and Body Language (from Lesson 1)

Connection *We have been developing our discussions by using the purposeful conversational moves and body language of strong speakers and listeners.*

Guided Interaction *When we have discussions, we ponder our ideas about the text—we "hang out" with them for a while. We think and talk about an idea from different angles.*

As we talk, our ideas take shape. As we continue to read, we gather more evidence to support or revise our thinking. As we accumulate evidence, we develop theories. Theories are big ideas based on accumulating evidence.

Today, we are going to read [story title]. As I read aloud, you follow along in your mind. Listen to your thinking and create images in your head to get inside the story. After we read the first section, we will share our initial ideas.

[Read the first section of text aloud, and pose a question.]

- (open) *So what are you thinking?*
- (direct) *What are you thinking about _____?*

[Solicit ideas by inviting students to share their thinking.]

- *Who else is thinking that? Look at all the people who share that smart thinking.*
- *Who has a different idea? Tell us more. Who else has this idea?*
- *Does anyone have another idea that we have not heard yet?*

[Summarize ideas.] *We have a few ideas on the table about [why the character is behaving a certain way, why the character might be thinking the way she is, and what the character will do under the circumstances]. How many of you are thinking [idea 1]? Who can talk more about that? What evidence do you have to support your thinking?*

The second idea on the table is ____. Who was thinking that? Who can say more about that? What evidence in the story makes you think that might be true?

[Scaffold discussion as necessary by prompting students to use conversational moves and body language.]

As I read the next section aloud, look for evidence to support or revise your thinking. As you gather evidence, you will develop your theory. [Read the next section of the story aloud and stop at an appropriate spot.] *Now what are you thinking? Take a moment and think about how to put into words what you are thinking with this additional information. Who would like to start us off?*

Send-Off

I would like you to finish reading this short piece of text with your partner. After you read it, talk quietly to each other about what you are thinking. When I see that partners have had the opportunity to talk, we will regroup and have a class discussion.

Group Wrap-Up

When you went off to finish the story, we had two theories on the table. [Review them.] *Now that you have had the opportunity to finish the story and discuss it with your partner, I am curious to hear what you are thinking. Remember to use the conversational moves and body language of strong speakers and listeners to help our discussion deepen. Who wants to start?*

[Prompt students to include evidence to support their thinking.]

- *Show us where in the story you found that evidence.*
- *What did the character say that shows this?*
- *Help us find that part of the text. Say it like this: "Go to the last paragraph on page ____."*
- *What additional evidence do you have to support that theory?*
- *Is there evidence that challenges that idea? What page is it on?*

LESSON 6

Language You Can Use to Connect Ideas During Discussion

Special Notes None

Thinking Behind the Lesson Students can better connect their ideas with the ideas of others if they have been introduced to some standard transitional phrases.

Materials

One copy of a short, engaging story for each student

A transparency of the story (optional)

Anchor chart: Conversational Moves and Body Language (from Lesson 1)

A talkmark for each student (see sample on page 54)

Connection *We have been having some wonderful discussions during our interactive read-alouds, but sometimes our ideas don't connect. People are sharing their ideas, but they are not connecting these ideas to what other people are saying.*

Guided Interaction *Today, I want to teach you some of the language that you can use to enter a discussion, share your ideas, piggyback on someone else's idea, share a new idea, and connect your ideas to what is being said. I'm going to give each of you a* talkmark *containing phrases you might use to participate in the discussion.*

When you are trying to enter the discussion, you might say:

- *Something I was thinking about was _____.*
- *I noticed that _____. I was wondering why _____.*
- *I think _____.*
- *I did not understand the part about _____.*

When you want to add to an idea someone else brought up, you might say:

- *I heard you say _____ and I agree because _____.*
- *I agree with your idea, and I think _____ is more evidence that supports it.*

When you want to bring up a different idea, you might say:

- *I understand that you think _____, but I have a different theory, which is that _____.*

When you don't understand or want clarification, you could say:

- *I don't understand what you mean. Could you please explain your thinking?*
- *Why do you think that? What evidence do you have to support that thinking?*

Using these phrases will help you think about entering the discussion and connecting your ideas with the ones on the table. As we read and discuss the story, practice saying these phrases. Think of other phrases you might use to enter or connect to the conversation.

[Read aloud the first two-thirds of the story interactively. Scaffold the discussion as needed. Prompt students to use phrases from their talkmark to enter or connect with the discussion.]

Send-Off *I would like you to finish reading this text with your partner. After you read it, talk quietly to each other about what you are thinking. When I see that partners have had a chance to talk, we will regroup and have a class discussion.*

Group Wrap-Up *When you began reading on your own, there were two [three] ideas on the table.* [Summarize the ideas.] *Now that you have completed the story, what are you thinking? Who would like to get our discussion started? Remember to use purposeful conversational moves and body language to promote a weblike discussion. You have a responsibility to promote the discussion, not just report your ideas. Use the phrases on your talkmark to help you enter the discussion or connect your ideas to other people's ideas.*

[Scaffold the discussion and prompt students to use the talkmark phrases as needed.]

Talkmark

To enter the discussion:

- Something I was thinking about was ____.
- I noticed that ____.
- I was wondering why ____.
- I think ____.
- I did not understand the part about ____.

To add to an idea:

- I heard you ____, and I agree because ____.
- I agree with your idea, and I think ____ is more evidence that supports it.
- I was thinking the same thing.
- I want to piggyback on what ____ was saying.

To bring up a different idea:

- I understand that you think ____, but I have a different idea, which is that ____.

When you want clarification:

- I do not understand what you mean. Could you please explain your thinking?
- Why do you think that? What in the text makes you think that?
- What evidence do you have to support that thinking?

Talkmark

To enter the discussion:

- Something I was thinking about was ____.
- I noticed that ____.
- I was wondering why ____.
- I think ____.
- I did not understand the part about ____.

To add to an idea:

- I heard you ____, and I agree because ____.
- I agree with your idea, and I think ____ is more evidence that supports it.
- I was thinking the same thing.
- I want to piggyback on what ____ was saying.

To bring up a different idea:

- I understand that you think ____, but I have a different idea, which is that ____.

When you want clarification:

- I do not understand what you mean. Could you please explain your thinking?
- Why do you think that? What in the text makes you think that?
- What evidence do you have to support that thinking?

FIGURE 11 Talkmarks

LESSON 7

Listening Actively

Special Notes This lesson can be videotaped and played again as necessary.

Thinking Behind the Lesson Knowing how to listen actively enables each student to be present in a discussion.

Materials

One copy of a short, engaging story for each student

A transparency of the story (optional)

Three-column anchor chart: Active Listening: Looks Like/Sounds Like/Feels Like

Before the Lesson Preselect two students who will observe the conversation and take notes.

Connection

We have been reading and discussing stories. You are learning to use the conversational moves and body language of strong listeners and speakers.

[Refer to the anchor chart "Conversational Moves and Body Language," begun in Lesson 1.]

Guided Interaction

Today, I want you to think about how you know when someone is really listening to you. What does it look like, sound like, and feel like when someone is actively listening to what you are saying?

I know that when I am talking and my daughter is really listening to me, her head nods and the expression in her eyes and on her face changes as she thinks about what I am saying. Often she says, "Uh-huh," or "Hmmm." Sometimes her eyebrows scrunch together, and that makes me think she doesn't agree with what I'm saying. Feeling my daughter's eyes looking at me helps me know she is really listening.

[Begin a three-column chart headed "Active Listening."]

Active Listening

Looks Like	Sounds Like	Feels Like
• Listener nods	• Listener says, "Uh-huh"	• Speaker is aware of listener's eyes
• Listener makes facial expressions (smiles, frowns)		
• Listener follows speaker with eyes		

We are going to read [story title]. As you hear my voice reading aloud, actively follow and think along in your mind. Then we'll discuss what we've read. I have asked [name and name] to jot down what they notice about what people look like and sound like when they are actively listening.

[Read the story aloud, stopping at a few appropriate spots to raise and discuss theories. While the group is reading and discussing, the two observers will note the behavior and verbal signals of people who are actively listening.]

[After the text is completed, have the observers share their notes with the class. Record observations on the three-column chart.]

[Invite the whole class to share what it noticed during the discussion.] *What did you see, hear, and feel when you were the speaker? What did you notice yourself doing as a listener? What did you notice about other people during the discussion?* [Record these ideas on the anchor chart.]

Send-Off *Today, when you read, actively listen to your thinking as you develop theories about the characters and their situations. I am looking forward to hearing about your reading during our conferences.*

Group Wrap-Up *We are becoming more and more aware of the moves and behavior of strong speakers and listeners. Each of you has the power and the responsibility to pay attention, to listen so that you can be open to ideas and expand your thinking. If you find your attention wandering, use one of the active listening strategies we identified so that you can listen more intently.*

LESSON 8

Collecting Evidence: Jotting Thinking on Sticky Notes or in the Margins

Special Notes Model using each tool separately; spread the lesson over several days.

Thinking Behind the Lesson Holding on to thinking while reading teaches students to keep track of their ideas and prepare for a discussion. It also keeps them engaged in their reading.

Materials One copy of a short, engaging story for each student

An enlarged copy or transparency of the story

Connection *We have been going deeper into reading and discussing text by pondering ideas and developing theories about characters and their situations.*

Guided Interaction *Today, I want to show you how I collect evidence to support my theories by jotting a few key words in the margin [on a sticky note]. As I read and find evidence, I will jot a few key words in the margin [on a sticky note] to help me remember that information and where it is located. My notes will help me refer to my evidence during discussion.*

Today, I selected a short story titled _____. I made an enlarged copy so that we can read together. Watch how I use the margins [sticky notes] to quickly jot notes to help me hold on to my thinking.

[Begin to read text aloud. Model stopping to jot notes about your thinking.] *Hmmm. I am starting to think that _____. I think this because right here it says _____, and _____, and _____. I'm going to write [the appropriate phrase] in the margin [on a sticky note] to hold on to my initial thinking.*

[Read aloud the next section of the story. Stop and think aloud how you jot notes in the margin or on a sticky note that support or revise your initial thinking.]

Send-Off *I would like you to finish reading this story with your partner. After you read it, talk quietly with each other about what you are thinking and make notes in the margins [on sticky notes]. When I see that partners have had the opportunity to talk, we will gather as a group and have a class discussion.*

Group Wrap-Up *When you went off to read independently, we had discussed a couple of ideas and theories.* [Review them.] *Now that you have finished the story and discussed it with your partner, I am curious about what you are thinking. As we talk, remember to use purposeful conversational moves and body language to help our discussion go deeper. Also use your notes to remind you of your thinking.*

So what are you thinking? Who would like to start us off?

[Prompt students to include evidence to support their thinking.]

- *Show us where in the story you found that evidence.*
- *Did the character say or do something that makes you think that?*
- *Where in the text did you find that evidence? Take us to that place in the text.*
- *What additional evidence do you have to support that theory?*
- *Is there evidence that challenges that idea? Show us where.*

LESSON 9

Developing Theories About Characters

Special Notes None

Thinking Behind The Lesson Developing theories about characters keeps readers engaged and thinking about the big ideas in the text.

Materials

One copy of a short, engaging story for each student

A transparency of the story (optional)

A display copy of Learning About the Character recording sheet (Appendix K), as well as an individual copy for each student

Connection *We know readers develop theories while they read. Theories are big ideas based on accumulating evidence.*

Guided Interaction

Readers develop theories about characters and the kinds of persons they are. We think, "I think this is the kind of character who is ____, and here's why I think that." We develop theories about why characters behave a certain way.

We develop theories about how characters are shaped by their circumstances.

Today, I'm going to read aloud [story title]. The main character is named ____. [Briefly introduce the character.] *As I read aloud, follow along silently. As we read, we will gather information that will tell us things about the character. Listen to your thinking and create an image of this person in your mind. Visualize the character and the way he looks, talks, behaves, thinks, moves. Paying attention to the things other characters think and say about him will help you do this.*

Watch how I find evidence to form an initial theory about the character and the kind of person he is. [Read the first section of the story aloud and share your initial ideas about the character.] *I'm thinking that this character is ____ because, right here, when he said [did] ____, it made me think ____.*

Do you see how I am collecting evidence about the character to help me form an initial theory that he is greedy [intelligent, independent, determined, proud, defiant]? It's an initial theory because a theory is based on accumulating evidence. We need to meet a character in a variety of situations to gather more information. I am going to jot this information on my recording sheet to support my thinking during discussion.

As we read the next section of the story together, jot down any information you find to support your theory on your recording sheet. You can refer to it when we stop to discuss the text. [Read the next section of the story aloud as students follow along silently.]

Now what are you thinking about the character and what makes you think that? Turn and talk with your partner about what you are thinking and what information from the text makes you think that. [Listen to the discussions; identify two or three common theories to share with the group.]

I heard two different theories. The first one is that the character is ____ because ____. How many readers are thinking the same thing? The second theory I heard was ____. How many readers are thinking that?

OK, we have two theories to discuss. Who can get us started with the first theory? Who feels ____ and would like to tell us why?

Do you see how we can have different theories even when we are reading the same book? Readers with different background knowledge form different theories. They may interpret a situation in a different way. Listening to each other helps us think about ideas in different ways and expands our thinking.

Send-Off

Today, during independent reading, you and your partner will finish reading the story together. Pay attention to evidence about the way the main character looks, talks, behaves, thinks, and moves and what other characters think and say about him. Stop and jot down your thinking in the margins [on your recording sheet] to hold on to it. Once you have finished the story, reread your notes and practice sharing your thinking with your reading partner.

Group Wrap-Up

[Review what the class discussed before students began reading independently.]

Now that you have had the opportunity to finish the story and discuss it with your partner, I am curious to hear what you are thinking. Who would like to begin?

[Prompt students to include evidence from their recording sheets to support their thinking.]

LESSON 10

Developing Theories About Characters' Behavior

Special Notes None

Thinking Behind the Lesson Analyzing characters' behavior in different situations keeps readers engaged and aware of a story's big idea.

Materials One copy of a short, engaging story for each student

A transparency of the story (optional)

Connection *We have been developing theories about characters in the stories we read.*

We develop these theories based on the way the character talks, how he or she behaves, and how he or she treats other people. We say, "I think this character is ____, and here's why." As we read more and more of the story, we accumulate evidence that revises or strengthens our theory.

Guided Interaction *Today, we are going to develop theories about why characters behave the way they do in various situations. How a character behaves in a situation depends on*

- *the character's background and prior experiences*
- *how the character feels he or she is being treated*
- *what the character wants to accomplish*

How we interpret a character's behavior depends on our background knowledge and our interpretation of the situation. If I see a girl teasing another girl, I might interpret this behavior as being mean, but it may be that the girls are friends playing a game.

Today I'm going to read [story title]. We will use what we know about [character's name] to discuss how she behaves in or reacts to a particular situation.

[Read the first section of the story aloud. Invite students to share their initial theories about the character.] *Let's think about what we have learned about the character so far. Turn and tell your partner what you are thinking about [character's name].*

[Listen as partners discuss and identify two or three common ideas.] *I heard two [three] possible theories about this character. How many of you are thinking ____? How many of you are thinking ____? Hold on to your idea as we continue to read and collect information to support or revise your thinking.*

[Continue to read until the character has to make a decision or behaves in a questionable way.] *Why do you think the character behaved that way? What do you know about the character that suggests she would behave that way?*

Turn and talk with your partner.

[Listen to the partnership discussions, and identify two or three common theories. Scaffold oral language for students having difficulty articulating their theories.] *So you think the character will probably ____ because ____. Say it like that. Practice saying it to your partner.*

I heard two different theories. The first is something about ____ because of ____. How many readers are thinking the same thing? Who can put this thinking into words? Who can extend that theory with additional evidence?

The second theory I heard was ____. Who can put this thinking into words? Who can extend that theory with additional evidence?

[Prompt discussion and summarize thinking as needed.]

Do you see how we each can have different theories even when we are reading the same book? That's because readers with different backgrounds have different ideas. Listening to each other helps us think about ideas in a different way. Readers revise their thinking and theories as they read.

Send-Off *I want you to finish reading this short story on your own. Be sure to jot your thinking and evidence in the margins [on sticky notes] to hold on to your thinking. Once you have finished the story, reread your notes and think about how you can put your ideas into words. Be prepared to share at the end of reader's workshop.*

Group Wrap-Up [Review what the class discussed before students began reading independently.]

Now that you have had the opportunity to finish the story and discuss it with your partner, what are you thinking? Who would like to share? Remember to use conversational moves and body language to help deepen our discussion.

[Prompt students to include evidence to support their thinking.]

- *Show us where in the story you found that evidence.*
- *Tell the readers to go to that part of the text. Say it like this: "Go to the last paragraph on page ____."*
- *What additional evidence do you have to support that theory?*
- *Is there any evidence that challenges this idea? Show us where.*

LESSON 11

Revising and Developing Thinking: Finding the Right Words

Special Notes None

Thinking Behind the Lesson Saying something the first time is a first draft of our thinking. We sharpen our language by sharing and discussing ideas with others.

Materials

One copy of a short, engaging story for each student

A transparency of the story (optional)

A clipboard and paper for each student

Connection *We have been discussing short stories by developing theories around big ideas. We have also been practicing using conversational moves and body language as a class and with partners.* [Refer to anchor chart "Conversational Moves and Body Language," begun in Lesson 1.]

Guided Interaction

Today, I am going to show you how you can revise and develop your initial idea. Our ideas change based on rereading and uncovering new information and by listening to someone else's ideas. Strong readers change their thinking based on new information.

Strong readers and thinkers know it is wise to revise their thinking, not hold on to original ideas just because they don't want to admit they were wrong. Strong readers and thinkers are open to information that supports or changes their thinking.

While I read the first section of text aloud, follow along silently. We will stop at an appropriate spot to share our thinking. [Read the first section of the story aloud.] *So what are you thinking?*

[Guide the discussion until two or three ideas surface.]

So we have a few ideas on the table. Write down what you are thinking on your clipboard. You can start like this: "I think such and such, and here is why I think that," or "I am thinking so and so. Evidence to support my thinking is thus and such." When you are finished, draw a line under your initial thinking.

[Give students a few minutes to quickwrite their initial ideas.]

Now we will read the next part of the story. Follow along in your mind and search for information that will develop or revise your initial ideas. [Stop at a point in text where students will have gathered supporting or conflicting information.]

Now what are you thinking? Why do you think that? Write down your theory below the line you drew under your initial idea. Write like you are talking. You can start like this: "I think so and so. My evidence is thus and such." When you are finished, draw a line under your new thinking. [Give students time to write.]

Look at your writing. Did your ideas grow after reading more of the text? How did your writing change? Did you add new information? Did you change your thinking? Was it easier to write and share your thinking? [Briefly discuss with students anything they notice about their writing.]

I'm going to read more of the story. When I stop again, we can continue to discuss the story and what we are thinking. [Read more of the story aloud. Ask an open question.] *So what are you thinking?* [Scaffold the discussion as necessary.]

[Select a couple of ideas that are taking shape.] *We have two ideas on the table about [why the character is behaving a certain way; why the character might be thinking something; what the character will do under the circumstances]. How many of you are thinking [the first idea]? The second idea is _____.*

As we discuss the two theories, listen to what other people are saying. Sometimes someone says something and we think, "Hmmm, that could be true. I didn't think of that." Sometimes someone says something that supports what we are thinking. We think, "That's another reason I didn't think of."

OK, who wants to start?

[When the discussion tapers off, share what you have noticed.]

Now that we have discussed the story so far, once again write down your theory. Start at the beginning and be sure to include all the information you have gathered from the reading and from listening to other ideas.

Look at your writing. Did your ideas grow after reading more of the text? How did your writing change? Did you add new information? Did you change your thinking? Was it easier to write and share your thinking? [Briefly discuss with students anything they notice about their writing.]

Send-Off *I want you to finish reading the story independently and then write down your final thinking. Now that you have talked and written about your initial ideas, you should have an easier time explaining your final theory. Write as if you are talking with your reading partner. The words you say are the words you write. Bring what you write with you when we wrap up today's workshop.*

Group Wrap-Up *Today, you are going to read your final thinking to your partner. You have had the opportunity to ponder and revise your ideas. Read and share your idea with a strong voice. Don't be afraid to revise a bit more as you speak. You can always write down that information later.*

[Gather the class for a final reflection.] *We've been pondering our ideas in order to revise and develop our thinking. What did you learn about yourself as a speaker today? What helped you develop your ideas until you found just the right words? How did your writing change? Does your writing sound like you? Did you write the words you said?*

Remember, it takes time to develop strong thinking, to develop a theory. Strong thinkers and speakers talk, read, and think to develop their initial ideas into theories. Talking about our ideas helps us revise and develop our initial thinking.

LESSON 12

Discussing Themes

Special Notes This lesson takes two days. The first day you use a familiar story; the second day, a new one.

Thinking Behind the Lesson Understanding and discussing theme is another opportunity to engage with the big ideas of a text.

Materials Day 1: the same story the students read in Lesson 11

Day 2: one copy of a short, engaging story for each student

A transparency of both stories (optional)

Connection *We have been developing theories about characters and the situations in which they find themselves.*

Guided Interaction *Today, I want to talk to you about* theme*—the big idea or lesson about life that the author wants us to think about after we read the story. The theme is the underlying message of the story.*

The author doesn't simply state the theme. You infer theme by thinking, "What is the lesson about life the author wants me to ponder? After reading this book, what lesson can I bring to how I live my life?"

There isn't always just one theme in a book. Readers may find different themes because, as we know, we think about and interpret stories based on our background knowledge and experiences.

Day 1

In our last lesson we read [story title] and discussed what kind of person the main character was and why she behaved the way she did. The story is about [retell/summarize it], but the important idea about life—the theme—that the author wants us to think about is ____. [Write the theme at the top of a piece of chart paper.]

The author doesn't come right out and tell us the theme. We have to connect clues—or evidence—from the text to infer and synthesize the theme. It's something we figure out either while we are reading or after we are done and are reflecting on the book. Let's hear some of your ideas about what the theme of this story is. What makes you think so?

Day 2
Today, we are going to read and discuss [title of story not read before]. We will stop from time to time to discuss what we have read and think about the theme.

[Read the whole story aloud, stopping for discussion at various points.]

Send-Off

Day 1
For the rest of the workshop, flip through the text and think aloud with your partner about how the events in the story help you synthesize the theme, like this: "This part when such and such happened, and then when she said that, made me think about so and so."

Day 2
On your own, reread the story and think about the theme—the lesson about life that the author is sharing. Remember, there may be several themes you can take away from a story. Ponder the text. What happened in the story? What did the character learn? What lesson is this story sharing about life? Write down your idea and explain why you think the way you do. You might say it like this:

"The theme I found in the story was such and so. I think this because . . ." and state your reasons and evidence. When you are finished, talk quietly with your partner and share your thinking.

Both Days
Once partners have had the opportunity to talk, we will regroup and discuss the themes you found.

[Listen to partnership discussions and assess students' ability to infer and synthesize a theme. Identify a few common themes they have found.]

Group Wrap-Up *Now that you are finished reading and rereading the text, what theme or lesson about life does it leave you thinking about? As I listened in on your conversations, I heard a few ideas. One idea was _____. Who would like to share their thinking about that theme?*

[Discuss various themes students have inferred from the text. Discuss how people interpret stories in different ways.]

Every reader has different background knowledge. How we interpret a story, a character, or a situation—the lesson we find—depends on our unique background knowledge and experiences.

LESSON 13

Sharpening Language and Articulating Thinking by Talking with a Partner

Special Notes None

Thinking Behind the Lesson Talking with someone else gives us an opportunity to deepen our initial ideas and sharpen the language we use to express them.

Materials One copy of a short, engaging story for each student

A transparency of the story (optional)

Connection *We know that readers develop theories while they read and discuss text. We know that these theories are ideas based on accumulating evidence. We develop and revise our ideas as we continue to read and discuss our thinking with others.*

Guided Interaction *Sharing ideas with a partner helps us sharpen our language and articulate our thinking. When we articulate our thinking, we feel comfortable with our ideas. We are able to explain our ideas clearly with precise language and evidence.*

When you share with your reading partner, you have a chance to practice explaining your ideas. You have time to get comfortable with the words so that you can share your thinking in an articulate way. Strong speakers talk about their initial ideas so they can find just the right words to explain their thinking.

Today, we will read and discuss another story together, as we have been doing throughout this unit. Pay particular attention to how your voice becomes stronger and how your words become clearer as we discuss the story together.

[Read the first section of the story aloud. Ask an open question.] *So what are you thinking? Who can start us off?* [Invite students who volunteer to share. Notice how many students are willing to share off the top of their heads.]

Many of us feel comfortable about sharing right away. I noticed that several people jumped right in. Others chose not to volunteer, and that's fine. You may be the kind of speaker who listens

first. Or you may be the kind of speaker who likes to practice thinking through what you will say so the words become comfortable.

Now share your thoughts about what we've read so far with your partner. [Listen to the partner discussions. There should be a noticeable buzz.]

I notice that when partners are working together, the class is always buzzing with talk. Everyone has something to say. But when I ask you to share your thinking with the whole group, often only a few students are willing to share. Some of you may want to ponder your ideas and practice sharing what you will say first.

Talking about our ideas with a partner gives us time to practice sharing our thoughts so that we can articulate our thinking.

Send-Off

I would like you to finish reading this short story with your partner. After you read it, talk quietly to each other about what you are thinking. When I see that partners have had the chance to talk, we will regroup and have a class discussion.

Group Wrap-Up

[Review the ideas that were discussed before students went off to work with their partners.]

Now that you have had the opportunity to finish the story and discuss it with your partner, I am curious about what you are thinking. Who would like to start us off?

[Lead a class discussion on how talking about our ideas helps us sharpen our language and articulate our thinking.]

- *Is it easier to explain your ideas after talking about them with a partner? Why is that?*
- *How did talking with your partner help you find just the right words to explain your thinking?*
- *Did your words flow more smoothly the more you talked?*

LESSON 14

Saying It So You Can Write It

Special Notes None

Thinking Behind the Lesson Teaching students the progression from talking to writing shows them that once you articulate your ideas aloud, writing and revising become more natural.

Materials One copy of a short, engaging text for each student

A blank transparency

Connection *We have been having wonderful discussions in which we've developed our initial ideas into theories supported by evidence. You know how to collect evidence by jotting in the margins or on sticky notes. You know that strong thinkers shape and revise their initial theories as they gather evidence. You know how to use conversations with another person to shape your thinking.*

Guided Interaction *Today, I want to show you that if we can say it, we can write it. We can talk with someone else about our ideas to practice articulating our thinking—to find just the right words.*

The words we write are not special—they're the same words we say. If I can tell you my theory about a character or her or his situation, then I can write it. Earlier in this unit we read [story title]. We had a wonderful discussion and came up with two theories about [character's name].

Who can share one of those theories with the class? [Choose a volunteer, and use what he says to model the process.] *Watch how I take the words you said and write them down so I can share your theory in writing. You said ____.* [Write the student's words on overhead.] *Now I will reread what I wrote to make sure it makes sense and I didn't miss anything.*

The other theory we came up with was about ____. Turn and talk with your partner and put that into words. Who can share that theory with the class? [Once again model writing down the spoken words.] *Do you see that if you can say it, you can write it?*

Now as a class we are going to read and discuss a story called ____. We will develop theories about the characters or their situations using evidence from the text. We will jot notes in the margins as we read along. We will revise and strengthen our theories as we continue to read. [Begin the interactive read-aloud.]

Send-Off *Today, while you are working on your own, I want you to ponder your final theory. Write down the points you want to make so that you will be able to articulate your thinking clearly.*

Then practice sharing your ideas with a partner. When you find just the right words, write them down. Remember, the words you say are the words you write. Reread your writing to make sure it makes sense and that you didn't forget anything.

Group Wrap-Up [Have students read their final thinking. Have several students share their writing.]

LESSON 15

Assessing a Discussion

Special Notes This lesson can be introduced earlier in the trajectory and repeated as needed.

Thinking Behind the Lesson Reflecting on a discussion helps each participant assess her own strengths and weaknesses and allows the group to set goals for future discussions.

Materials One copy of a short, engaging story for each student

Before the Lesson Preselect a few students who will observe the class discussion and record their observations.

Connection *We have been learning the purposeful conversational moves and body language of strong speakers and listeners.* [Review the anchor chart "Conversational Moves and Body Language," begun in Lesson 1.]

Guided Interaction *Today, we are going to read and discuss another story. I have asked a few class members to record what they notice about our discussion. After we discuss this text, they will share what they noticed.*

Today, we will read and discuss [story title]. During our discussion, remember your job as a strong speaker and listener. If you see that a classmate has not had an opportunity to talk, invite him or her into the discussion.

[Read the first section of the story aloud. Stop at an appropriate spot that is likely to invite discussion.] *So what are you thinking? Who can start the discussion?*

[Stand aside and allow the discussion to flow without prompting. When the discussion tapers off, have the observers share their notes. List these observations on chart paper so that the class can hold on to them. Help the class reflect on these behaviors.] *What can we say about our discussions based on these observations? Who purposefully used a conversational move or some attentive body language? Think about what you can learn about yourself as a speaker and listener?*

Send-Off

Now, as you work on your own, I want you to reflect on yourself as a speaker and a listener. What are your strengths? Refer to our class anchor chart "Conversational Moves and Body Language." Identify two strengths and two goals for yourself as a speaker and listener. If you have never invited someone into the discussion, that could be a goal.

If you see that you talk a lot during discussions, think about a move you can use to invite others to join in. Write down your two goals and conversational moves you can use to achieve them. Be prepared to share at our workshop wrap-up.

Group Wrap-Up [Have the students write two discussion goals they will work on in their journals.]

LESSON 16

Finding Ways to Disagree Respectfully: Challenging and Debating Ideas

Special Notes

This lesson is for students who are comfortable with discussion and ready to deal with some of the finer points.

Thinking Behind the Lesson

Students need to learn language they can use to push thinking beyond polite agreement—to disagree without dismissing someone else's idea.

Materials

One copy of a short, engaging text for each student

Anchor chart: Ways to Disagree Respectfully (prepare this chart ahead of time)

Anchor chart: Conversational Moves and Body Language (from Lesson 1)

Connection

I've been noticing that you're not always sure how to disagree with someone and still keep the discussion going in a friendly way. However, debating and challenging each other's ideas is an important part of a discussion.

Guided Interaction

Today, I want to talk about ways to challenge and debate someone when we don't agree with what she or he has said. It's important to express our disagreement in a respectful way if we want our opinions to be heard.

Here's a chart listing things you might say if someone says something you don't agree with [refer to the chart you've previously prepared]:

- *First, acknowledge what someone else has said.*
- *Then say, "I'm not sure I agree with that. Can you tell me what in the story gave you that idea?"*
- *Finally, say, "I have a different idea," and state your opinion.*

If we agree to disagree respectfully, nobody has to feel afraid to share his or her ideas. Remember that all ideas are valued and we can learn from each other. [Add that "all ideas are valued" to the "Conversational Moves and Body Language" chart.]

Let's think about how we can challenge each other without being mean or sounding angry. First, consider what you want to say and then think about how you can say it in a respectful way.

Turn to a partner and instead of saying, "That's not right!" restate your idea in a respectful way. [Add any new ideas to the "Ways to Disagree Respectfully" chart.]

[Read the first two-thirds of today's story aloud interactively. Scaffold the discussion as needed. Prompt students to disagree with respectful language.]

Send-Off

I want you to finish reading the rest of this short story on your own. To prepare for today's wrap-up, jot notes in the margin, come up with some talking points for your ideas and theories, and practice articulating your final thinking.

Group Wrap-Up

So, what are you thinking? Remember to use the discussion moves and body language of strong speakers and listeners to deepen our discussion. Who would like to begin?

[Guide the group discussion, paying particular attention to respectful disagreement.]

Remember, strong speakers disagree respectfully. They present their ideas in a way that promotes the discussion.

LESSON 17

Using Talking Points

Special Notes This lesson is for students who are comfortable with discussion and ready to deal with some of the finer points.

Thinking Behind the Lesson Creating talking points to support your theory helps you articulate your thinking.

Materials One copy of a short, engaging story for each student

A blank transparency

Connection *We know that readers develop theories while they read and discuss text and that these theories are built on evidence.*

Guided Interactiion *It can be difficult to remember all the important points you want to share during a discussion. Strong speakers use talking points to help them. Talking points are key words and phrases that help you remember important ideas and evidence that you want to include as you share your thinking.*

Today, we will read and discuss [story title] as we usually do. When we finish, I am going to show you how I jot down talking points to explain my final theory.

[Read the story aloud interactively. Prompt students to use conversational moves and body language as needed.]

Now that we have completed and discussed the story, I have developed my final theory about it. Watch and listen as I think about my theory aloud to prepare to share my final thinking. As I'm thinking aloud, I'm going to jot down the key words and evidence I want to be sure to include.

[Think aloud and, on a transparency, model listing the key points and evidence that will prompt you as you explain your thinking. When the list is completed, model using the talking points to articulate your ideas clearly.]

Send-Off

Today, I want you to reread this short story and develop your final theory about it. Think how you will put your ideas into words. While you think aloud, make a list of talking points you want to be sure to include. Practice using your talking points to explain your thinking to your partner. As you share, add any points that you missed on the original list.

Be prepared to share when we wrap up today's workshop.

Group Wrap-Up [Have students, in small groups or as a whole class, use their talking points to articulate their final theories.]

LESSON 18

Inviting Others into the Discussion

Special Notes None

Thinking Behind the Lesson Everybody is responsible for ensuring that all voices are heard during a discussion.

Materials One copy of a short, engaging story for each student

Anchor chart: Conversational Moves and Body Language (from Lesson 1)

Connection *We have been talking about purposeful discussion moves and body language. We know that a strong discussion is weblike.*

Guided Interaction *Strong speakers and listeners know that one of their jobs is to ensure that everyone feels welcome to share his or her ideas.*

Sometimes people have difficulty taking part in a discussion. You need to be aware when someone has not had a chance to talk and invite her or him to participate. You might say it like this, "[Name], What are you thinking?" or say, "What do you think about that, [name]? Do you agree?"

Everyone turn to your partner and practice these words. How else could you say it? [Lead a discussion of alternative language and add any additional suggestions to the anchor chart "Conversational Moves and Body Language."]

When you invite others to join in, it lets them know you care about their ideas. When you listen to someone else's ideas, it helps you refine your own. That person is also more likely to listen to your ideas if you've listened to his.

Now we'll read and discuss [story title]. During our discussion, remember your job as a strong speaker and listener. If you see that a classmate has not had an opportunity to talk, invite him or her to join in the discussion.

[Read two-thirds of the story aloud interactively. If necessary, prompt students to invite others into the discussion—whisper in their ear, *Say to [name], "What do you think about that?"]*

Send-Off *I would like you to finish reading this story on your own. After you read it, talk quietly with your partner about what you are thinking. When I see that partners have had the chance to talk together, we will regroup and have a class discussion.*

Group Wrap-Up *As we get ready to share what we thought about this story, remember to use the conversational moves and body language of strong speakers and listeners to deepen our discussion. Also remember your role as a strong speaker and listener. Invite others into the discussion.*

So what are you thinking? Who would like to start us off?

UNIT 3

Genre Study for Developing Sophisticated Nonfiction Readers

The recent shift toward teaching nonfiction literacy skills in addition to nonfiction content was triggered by Ellin Keene and Susan Zimmermann's book *Mosaic of Thought* (2007). Many types of writing fall into the category of nonfiction—among them how-to books, biographies and autobiographies, science and nature books, opinion articles and essays, and textbooks. We chose biography for our nonfiction unit of study because the way in which fourth graders make the transition from fiction to nonfiction is critical, and biographies are often written as narratives. More than other forms of nonfiction, biography has the potential to engage fourth graders on a variety of levels while allowing them to use their growing discussion skills.

Furthermore, we wanted this inquiry to go beyond researching and regurgitating facts. Students read biographies to learn, question, and develop theories about why these people have been written about in the first place and how what they have done influences our lives today. This kind of in-depth study engages fourth graders as readers and inspires them to learn

- why these people are considered important
- how they overcame obstacles to accomplish what they did
- how the time and place in which they lived influenced who they were, the decisions they made, and what they accomplished
- how they influenced people of their own time and subsequent times

We expect reading these biographies and meeting these people to affect the way students see themselves and live their lives.

Franki Sibberson, in an essay for Choice Literacy (www.choiceliteracy.com) titled "Nonfiction Books for Independent Reading: Moving Beyond Content

Connections," discusses how important it is to share nonfiction with our students beyond the reading they do for science or social studies. She reminds us that we want our students to read all kinds of books so that they can enjoy learning about life and the world from many and varied perspectives. Encouraging our students to maintain a healthy reading diet requires that biographies be part of the mix.

Steeping Yourself in the Genre

Before teaching any new genre, you need to immerse yourself in it in order to understand the structure, themes, and common characteristics and to anticipate the possible questions students may raise. Gather many different types of biography at varied levels of difficulty: picture books, essays, chapter books, short narrative sketches, articles, and so on. Be thoughtful about the ones you choose. Some are so watered-down as to have lost their literary integrity: they provide the skeletal information of a summary rather than a rich account that allows the reader to enter the life and times of the subject.

Designing the Unit of Study

There are a couple of ways to organize this study. One is to concentrate on a particular type of notable person—heroes, explorers, peacemakers, strong women, sports figures, for example. The other is to open it up to anyone and everyone. Either way, make sure to provide a variety and range of materials so that students will be able to find just-right texts they can read. Also, students should explore both historical and contemporary subjects so they don't think biographies are only about dead people. They need to see that there are movers and shakers with us in the world today.

We recommend that the focus lessons highlight a class subject. Text used in the explicit instruction and guided practice components of the lesson will focus on the highlighted subjects. After the immersion phase, students self-select subjects to study during Independent Practice.

The trajectory of this unit of study is based on the work of Isoke Titilayo Nia. We have also read books by Katie Wood Ray, Janet Angelillo, Sharon Hill and Judy Davis, and Lucy Calkins. These mentors have taught us how to do the preliminary research, identify the critical elements that must be included, develop explicit lessons, and still be responsive to the learners we have in front of us.

Beginning the Inquiry: Immersion

Once you have collected an array of texts that you feel meet the interests and readability levels of your students, you are ready to begin several days of immersion. During the immersion lessons, students become familiar with the genre, notice and name essential features and characteristics, and activate their prior knowledge. Rereading is an important part of the process: the more they look, the more they'll see. Don't cut this part short even if you feel pressed for time.

Digging Deeper

Moving on, students apply the active reading strategies they have learned during previous units of study. As they read, they lift information off the page and talk about what they are learning. Just as they did with fictional characters, they now develop theories about the character traits of real people. They discuss the obstacles and challenges these people have overcome and how other people in their lives have influenced the decisions they've made. They revise their thinking based on accumulating evidence, just as they did when reading fiction.

Synthesis

With the biographies they have read as a catalyst, students can now tackle the big ideas behind them: issues such as promoting peace and combating hunger, poverty, and violence. Reading about people who have overcome obstacles and knowingly faced danger inspires us to reconsider the choices we make. History is both a story about the past and a window into the present. The lives and histories we learn about by studying biographies influence the way we think and the way we live our lives.

IMMERSION			
LESSON 1	LESSON 2	LESSON 3	LESSON 4
Defining and Characterizing Biography	Recognizing Biography Formats	Choosing the Subject of a Biography	Reading for a Purpose: Selecting a Subject to Study
LESSON 5	LESSON 6		
Identifying and Using Text Features	Reading Biographies Actively		
DIGGING DEEPER			
LESSON 7	LESSON 8	LESSON 9A	LESSON 9B
Sifting Through the Details	Separating Important Information from Interesting Information	Using Chapter Book Structures to Help Us Understand Biography	Using Picture Book Structures to Help Us Understand Biography
LESSON 9C	LESSON 10	LESSON 11	LESSON 12
Using Article Structures to Help Us Understand Biography	Understanding the Influence of Time and Place	Understanding the Influence of Other People	Uncovering Character Traits
LESSON 13			
Identifying Motivations That Cause People to Act			
SYNTHESIS			
LESSON 14*	LESSON 15	LESSON 16	
Developing Theories About How a Subject's Accomplishments Changed Society's Perceptions and Attitudes	Inferring Common Theme	Understanding How Reading Biography Affects You as a Person	

As always, base the lessons you present and the order in which you do so on who your particular students are.

FIGURE 12 Unit Trajectory

LESSON 1

Defining and Characterizing Biography

Special Notes Present this lesson over a period of two or three days.

Select a subject for class to spotlight.

Thinking Behind the Lesson Giving students time to immerse themselves in the genre allows them to become comfortable and familiar with the format, structure, and characteristics. This will enable them to read strategically.

Materials A chapter book biography about the subject the class will spotlight

Anchor chart: Characteristics of Biography

Characteristics of Biography

A collection of biographies (in labeled containers) that includes a range of readability levels, subjects, and types

Connection *You know that texts are categorized by genre. We have been reading and thinking deeply about fiction—stories with characters, settings, and plots.*

Explicit Instruction *Today, we are going to begin a new unit of study on biography. Like fiction or poetry, biography is a genre—a type of book with particular characteristics. Learning about different genres is important because it exposes us to books we might not ordinarily be interested in reading.*

For the next few days, we will be taking a close look at biographies to learn what a biography is and to identify different characteristics of this genre. To learn about any genre, you find information from the structure (the way the author organized the text), the words, the pictures, and other text features. We will study together. Later, you will select a subject you are interested in studying.

Before I read a book in a new genre, I flip through it, scanning it to see how it is organized. This helps me think about how I should read it. [Flip through the first few pages of text and name a couple of the characteristics you notice. Write your ideas on the class chart.]

The title tells me whom the biography is about. That is clear. There is a table of contents. This tells me that the book is organized by chapters. There are a lot of words on the page, like a fiction book. It looks like a story. There are photographs [illustrations] that help me visualize the person.

Now I will read a bit aloud and see what I learn about this genre from the words. [Read a couple of pages of the biography and name a couple characteristics.] *One thing I notice is that there is a chapter title in boldface type that says "Early Years." I'm thinking that I'm going to learn about what [subject name]'s life was like when he was young.* [Record this point on the class chart.]

Guided Practice *Now it's your turn. As I read the next couple of pages aloud, think about what you notice about the genre of biography. Remember, you can get information from the words, the pictures, and other features of the text.* [Read the next section aloud, stopping at a point where students will have noticed a few characteristics.] *Turn and share with your partner what you noticed about the genre of biography after reading that section. What did you notice about the content (the information the words told us), the structure, and the text features?*

[Once students have had the opportunity to share with their partners, lead a discussion of the characteristics they noticed. Name and record these characteristics on the class chart.]

Send-Off *Now I'm going to give each group a collection of biographies to look at.*

Browse these biographies and use sticky notes to record the characteristics that you notice. Be prepared to share your ideas during our wrap-up discussion.

Group Wrap-Up *What did you notice about the genre of biography? Let's go around the circle and each of you name something you noticed. If you don't have a different idea, it's OK to repeat something someone's already mentioned.*

[Record students' ideas on the class chart.]

Think about the books you've examined and the characteristics we have noted. Take a minute to find just the right words in a sentence or two to define a biography.

Now turn and talk with a partner and share your ideas. [Listen as students talk. Capture the collective thinking of the group and write down a working definition for biography. For example: A biography is a factual history of a person's life.]

LESSON 2

Recognizing Biography Formats

Special Notes None

Thinking Behind the Lesson Exposing students to various biography formats legitimizes them and ensures that all members of the community will be able to find material that is just right.

Materials A collection of biographies about the class subject in different formats: picture books, essays, articles, chapter books, poems, interviews

Three-column anchor chart: Biography Formats

Title	Format	Why I Want to Read This Book

A copy of the chart for each student

Connection *We know biographies are factual histories of people's lives.*

Guided Interaction *Biographies are written in many different ways. [Hold up a picture book.] The name of this book is ____. It's a picture book biography. I like reading picture books because I like how the illustrations in a picture book help me get inside the writing and create stronger sensory images. When I read a picture book, I learn some basic information, and if I am curious to know more, I can read a more detailed text.*

[Record your thinking on the class chart.]

[Hold up a chapter book.] *Here is a different kind of biography. Who would like to read a chapter book? Why? Why do you like to read this kind of book?* [Record responses on class chart.]

[You want students to know that it is OK to read picture books and shorter texts like articles, poems, and plays to learn about a person. This will allow you to differentiate reading materials based on students' abilities and interests.]

Send-Off

During independent reading, in pairs, browse through at least three different formats of biographies. Record your ideas on a three-column chart.

Think about yourself as a reader. What format of biography is of most interest to you?

Group Wrap-Up

[Have students share examples of the different biography formats they browsed. Discuss why a reader might read each type and what kind of information it provides. Add these ideas to the class chart.]

LESSON 3

Choosing the Subject of a Biography

Special Notes None

Thinking Behind the Lesson Understanding the author's purpose for selecting a subject or topic helps students begin to grapple with the bigger ideas of the genre.

Materials One copy of a short biographical text for each student

Containers of biographies in a variety of styles and reading difficulty: picture books, essays, articles, chapter books, poems, interviews, etc.

Three-column anchor chart: Obstacle/Accomplishment/Fascination

Obstacle	Accomplishment	Fascination

One copy of anchor chart for each student

Connection *Yesterday we began talking about the genre of biography and why we read biographies.* [Review the different types of biographies you discussed.]

Guided Interaction *Today we're going to think about why an author would choose to write about a particular person.*

Authors don't write about just anyone. An author might write about someone because he or she overcame obstacles to be successful [Helen Keller, Jackie Robinson, Babe Didrickson, etc.], or accomplished something important [an inventor], or is someone people are fascinated by [a movie star].

We're going to read an article called, "____"As we read, we're going to be thinking, "Did this person overcome an obstacle? Accomplish something important? Or did the author simply find this person fascinating?" If we find information about an accomplishment, an obstacle, or fascination, we'll jot some notes under that heading. [Think aloud as you read the first few paragraphs and record your thinking on the three-column anchor chart.]

Read the next paragraph with a partner. If you find information about an obstacle or an accomplishment or something that makes this person fascinating, make a note about it. [Invite students to share information they found and their reactions to it.]

Send-Off

Today you are going to finish this article by yourself (or with a partner) during independent reading. Continue to note any obstacles, accomplishments, or things that make this person fascinating on your three-column chart. Be prepared to share at the group wrap-up.

When you are finished, continue to browse through other biographies and think about why each author may have been motivated to write about that person.

Group Wrap-Up

Now that you have had the opportunity to complete the article, what additional information did you note about the obstacles, accomplishments, and things that make this person fascinating?

[Record students' ideas on the three-column chart. Lead the class in a final discussion about the author's motivation to write about this person.]

LESSON 4

Reading for a Purpose: Selecting a Subject to Study

Special Notes None

Thinking Behind the Lesson Setting a purpose helps readers focus their reading. The purpose may be interest, knowledge, or an assignment.

Materials A varied collection of biographies: picture books, essays, articles, chapter books, poems, interviews, etc.

Ways for students to record choices: sticky notes, reading journals, lined paper

Connection *We talked about why an author might choose to write about a certain person. The person may have overcome obstacles or accomplished something important, or perhaps the person is someone people find fascinating.*

Guided Interaction *As readers, we have individual interests. Today you're going to browse the collection of biographies I've assembled and select three people you would like to learn more about. For example, I know after having browsed through many of these biographies that I'd like to read about ____ because ____. I'll put that name on my list, along with the reason I am interested in reading and learning about this person. But I'm not sure whom else I'd be interested in reading about. I need to preview some other books to determine my other two choices.*

First, I'll look at the front and back covers to find information about the person and that text. Then I'll look at the table of contents to see whether there are topics that interest me and flip through the book and look at any photographs or illustrations.

[Show students how you spend time browsing through all the parts of the book before making a decision.]

Have you seen any biographies that interest you? Whom might you be interested in reading about? What makes that person interesting? [Invite students to discuss possible subjects to read about. (Asking students to select a person rather than a specific book will allow you to match them to a text at an appropriate readability level.)]

Send-Off *While you are working independently, browse through the collection of biographies and list three people you would like to read about and the reason you are interested in each of those people.*

Group Wrap-Up [Have students share.]

[Later, assign students one of their choices to study. Ensure that you can provide students with material at an appropriate level of difficulty.]

LESSON 5

Identifying and Using Text Features

Special Notes Students will begin reading text about their self-selected subject.

Thinking Behind the Lesson Readers need to understand the text features of biographies in order to comprehend them efficiently and effectively.

Materials The collection of biographies you've assembled for this unit

Two-column anchor chart: Biography Text Feature/How It Helps Me

Biography Text Feature	How It Helps Me

Connection *Biography is nonfiction; it is factual. We have looked at many different types of biographies, including picture books, chapter books, articles, and interviews. Nonfiction material like this includes certain features to help us understand it.*

Explicit Instruction *Today, we will begin studying some common features of biography and how they help us understand the text and gain more information. Biographies have some of the same text features we have seen in other kinds of nonfiction. For example, as I browse through this biography, I see* [choose those that apply and that you wish to address]:

- *a table of contents, which tells me in which chapters certain information can be found*
- *an index to help me find specific information quickly*
- *a glossary so that I can find out the meaning of unfamiliar terms*
- *visual images—illustrations and photographs—that help me understand the information being presented*

- *time lines, diagrams, maps, word bubbles, tables, charts, graphs, and boxed text that highlight and clarify information*
- *typographic features and special effects, such as titles, chapter headings, typefaces (boldface, italic), colored print, bullets, and captions, which also call attention to important information*

Guided Practice *With your partner, browse through two or three biographies about your subject and find some examples of text features. Think about how each feature helps the reader, and jot down your thoughts on a sticky note.*

[Have students share text features they have found and tell how they help the reader gain information. Record the ideas on a two-column chart.]

Send-Off *Today, while you're reading the biography you've chosen, place a sticky note next to any text features you find. Jot down the type of feature it is and how it helped you gain information. Be prepared to share when we wrap up the workshop.*

Group Wrap-Up [Have students share the text features in their biographies and how they help the reader. Record additional features and ideas on the two-column chart.]

LESSON 6

Reading Biographies Actively

Special Notes None

Thinking Behind the Lesson Readers can use known strategies to understand a new genre.

Materials A picture book biography or other short piece about class subject

Three-column anchor chart: Information Provided in the Text/Questions, Connections, Images, Inferences/My Thinking

Information Provided in the Text	Questions, Connections, Images, Inferences	My Thinking

Connection *We have been learning that reading is thinking. Strong readers pay attention to their inner conversation while they read, whether they're reading fiction or nonfiction, a novel, or a biography.*

Explicit Instruction *Today, I want to show you how I use strong, active reading strategies while reading a biography. I will listen to my inner conversation and make note of what I am thinking as I read. I will create sensory images, make connections, ask questions, and make inferences, just as I do whenever and with whatever I'm reading. OK, here I go.*

[Read the first section of the text aloud. Stop at an appropriate spot and share your thinking while you make the appropriate entries on the three-column chart. Use language like this: *Hmmm, that makes me wonder . . . Wow! I can just see . . . Oh, so when the subject was young, he . . . I think that probably . . . My inference here is . . .]*

Listening to my inner conversation helps me read actively so I get inside the text and am better able to understand and remember the information.

Guided Practice *All right, let's read the rest of this short biography together. As we read, listen to your inner conversation. Think about any questions you may have or any inferences you have made. Form images in your mind about what is going on with this person in his life.*

[Read the rest of the text, stopping at points where students will have questions, inferences, or visualizations to offer. Add these ideas to the three-column chart.]

Send-Off *Strong readers apply the same active reading strategies whatever the genre. While you read more of the biography you've chosen, pay attention to your inner conversation. Make a three-column chart and record your thinking.*

Group Wrap-Up [Have students share something they've learned about the people they're reading about by paying attention to their inner conversations.]

LESSON 7

Sifting Through the Details

Special Notes None

Thinking Behind the Lesson Readers need to know how to sift through the details and identify and retain what's important.

Materials A couple pages of text of class subject

A transparency of this chapter (optional)

Three-column anchor chart: Important Event/Details/My Thinking

Important Event	Details	My Thinking

Connection *We have been discussing biographies and analyzing their structure. We know biographies are often chronological accounts of important events in the subject's life. The author doesn't write about every single day in the person's life. The author selects important events that show what that person has accomplished or overcome.*

Explicit Instruction *Each chapter in a biography focuses on an important event in the person's life. The author describes the event by sharing details. The details explain why the event was powerful in shaping this person's life. As I read, I sift through these details and identify the ones I need to remember.*

Watch as I identify the important event and sift through the details about it. First, I will use the title of the chapter to see whether it will tell me what important event it will describe. Sometimes it tells me outright, and sometimes I have to read a bit of the chapter and infer what important event it's about.

[If the title states the event:] *Right here, it says ____. So I know this chapter is about that important event.*

[If the title is less obvious:] *The chapter title is ____. Hmmm. I know that this has something to do with ____, so the important event in this chapter is probably ____. But I'll need to read on to see if I am correct.* [Here's a specific example: *This chapter is called "Franklin Tames Lightning." Hmmm. I know that Benjamin Franklin learned about lightning while he was flying a kite. I bet the main idea of this chapter will be about that event.]*

Now I will read on to learn the details of what happened. [Read the first paragraph or two aloud. Then, thinking aloud, sift out the important details related to the event.] *Oh, so that is how this happened. I will write that here.* [Enter the information on the chart.]

[Read the next paragraph and again model sifting through the details that explain the important event.]

Watch how I use my notes to help me remember and explain what I have learned.

[Use the information on the chart to summarize what you've learned.]

Guided Practice *Let's read the next paragraph together. I will read aloud as you follow along in your mind. After we finish, we will sift through any supporting details that help us understand this important event.* [Read paragraph aloud. Have students turn and talk with partners.] *Discuss with your partner any important information that we read that helps explain the event.*

[Lead a class discussion to identify details that support (explain) the event. Have partners use class notes to explain what they have learned.

[Repeat several times until students demonstrate a growing understanding.]

Send-Off *Today, while you read more of the biography you have chosen, create a three-column chart in your reader's notebook to record important events and supporting details about the subject you are studying. Be prepared to share when we wrap up the workshop.*

Group Wrap-Up [Have students use their notes to explain what they have learned with their partner.]

LESSON 8

Separating Important Information from Interesting Information

Special Notes None

Thinking Behind the Lesson Being able to separate important information from interesting information helps students organize and retain knowledge.

Materials A biography of class subject

Three-column anchor chart from Lesson 7: Important Event/Details/My Thinking

Connection *We have been learning about biographies and what makes them different from other genres. We have analyzed how authors organize biographies. Many biographies are chronological presentations of important events in the subject's life. Yesterday we sifted out the main supporting details to help explain why the event was important.*

Explicit Instruction *Often biographies are written like a story. They describe important events as they would be told in a fictional story. The author includes a lot of details that make the person's life read like a novel. This information adds interest but is not necessarily needed to explain the importance of the person's life.*

Sometimes the author includes so many details that it is difficult to separate the important ones from the interesting ones. If my purpose for reading is to understand why this person was important, I am going to look for those kinds of supporting details.

Today, we are going to read [biography title]. From the title, I infer that the main event the author will be writing about is _____. I will search for supporting details that help me understand the event.

[Read one or two paragraphs aloud. Think aloud and share a supporting detail with the class.] *Hmm. I read that _____. That helps me understand why this time in this person's life was important. I will write that as a supporting detail.* [Add it to the chart. Then share a piece of interesting information.] *I also read that his brother _____. That is interesting, but it doesn't support why this event was important for this person. It is interesting, though. I will put that under "My Thinking." I will code it with an "I" for interesting.* [Add it to the chart.]

[Repeat this process two or three times until students demonstrate an increasing understanding.]

Watch how I use my notes to help me remember and explain what I have learned.

Guided Practice *I will read the next paragraph aloud as you follow along in your mind. When we finish, we will share any supporting details and interesting information that we found.* [Read aloud, stopping at an appropriate spot for students to collect their thinking and share.]

What did you learn that supports or explains why this event happened? What information helps you understand why this event helped shape this person's life? What is interesting information that helps the author tell the story? Can it be left out when we share information about this person [event]?

[Lead a class discussion in which students separate supporting details from interesting information. Record the information on chart.]

[Repeat as necessary, depending on students' understanding.]

Send-Off *Today, while you read more of the biography you have chosen, continue to collect important information in your reader's notebook. Code interesting information with an "I" under "My Thinking" to hold on to it.*

Group Wrap-Up [Have students use their notes to explain what they have learned and some interesting facts with their partner.]

LESSON 9A

Using Chapter Book Structures to Help Us Understand Biography

Special Notes None

Thinking Behind the Lesson Every biography format has specific structural features that help readers understand the text.

Materials A chapter book biography to use as an example

A transparency of the book's table of contents

Three-column anchor chart: Structure of Biographies: Type of Biography/Structure/How It Helps Me

Blank chart paper on which to create a time line

Connection *We have been studying biography, which is a specific kind of nonfiction—a true story (history) of a person's life. We also know that there are different formats for biographies, like picture books and chapter books.*

Explicit Instruction *Authors structure the information to help us understand. In a story we learn about the characters, the setting, the plot, and how things are resolved. Biographies have some of these same narrative features. The main character is the person the biography is about. The setting is the time and place the person lived. The plot is the story of the person's life.*

The structure of a biography is often chronological. It begins when the subject was a child and moves through his or her life in order as he or she gets older or accomplishes certain things.

A biography doesn't tell about every day of the person's life. Rather, the author identifies important events to share about the person. Having the events in a biography presented chronologically helps me understand the life of this person and how events influenced him or her. I can use this information to create a time line of important events.

Here is a chapter book biography about [person's name]. Look at the table of contents. The first chapter is [chapter title]. Do you see how it begins when the subject was young? [Begin a time line with the event or events dealt with in Chapter 1.] *Chapter 2 is [chapter title]. This must have been an important event in this subject's life for the author to write about it.* [Add this event to the time line.]

Guided Practice [Guide students as they discuss the remaining entries in the table of contents. Continue adding important events to the time line.] *Strong readers use the structure of the book to help them organize the information they are learning. For example, I know the events in this biography are presented chronologically. The author tells us about important events in [person's name]'s life in the order they happened so that we have a complete picture of what this person accomplished. I can make a time line of the important events in this person's life.*

[Record ideas on anchor chart.]

Structure of Biographies

Type of Biography	Structure	How It Helps Me
Chapter book	Chronological presentation of important events	I know the order in which things happened I can easily identify important events I can create a time line

Send-Off *As you work on your own today, I want you to think about how the author structured the biography you are reading. Is it chronological and based on important events in the subject's life? That's the most common approach, but yours might have a different structure. Use the structure of the book to help you organize the information you are learning.*

Group Wrap-Up [Have students share the different structures they noticed in the books they are reading.]

We are going to continue learning about the text structure of biographies and how we can use that structure to organize our learning.

LESSON 9B

Using Picture Book Structures to Help Us Understand Biography

Special Notes None

Thinking Behind the Lesson Every biography format has specific structural features that help readers understand the text.

Materials A picture book biography of spotlighted subject

Each student partnership will need a picture book of self-selected subject

Anchor chart: Structure of Biographies (from Lesson 9a)

Connection *Yesterday we discussed how chapter book biographies are often written in chronological order and are based on important events.*

Explicit Instruction *Today, we are going to analyze how picture book biographies are structured. How does the author organize the text to share the information?*

I am going to begin reading this picture book aloud. After a few pages I will stop and see what I know about how the author structured the text. [Read the first few pages aloud and share what you notice about the text structure. Two possibilities are suggested below.]

- *Hmmm. So this picture book began when he was ____ years old and now the subject is ____ years old. It seems that each page is about a different time and event in the subject's life. The author is moving in order and basing the story on important events, just like in a chapter book, but isn't telling as much about each event.*
- *I see. The author is just telling about one event when . . . This picture book is just about that one event.*

Guided Practice *Now let's look at another picture book together. I'll begin to read it aloud and you follow along in your mind. Think about who and what this biography is about and how the author structured the writing.*

[Begin to read aloud and stop at a spot where students will have gathered enough information to identify the content of the book and the structure of the writing.

Lead the students in a discussion of what they notice. Record their ideas about the structure of picture book biographies on the anchor chart.

Structure of Biographies

Type of Biography	Structure	How It Helps Me
Chapter book	Chronological presentation of important events	I know the order in which things happened I can easily identify important events I can create a time line
Picture book	Chronological presentation of important events; each page captures one event	I know the order in which things happened I can easily identify important events I can create a time line
Picture book	Description of one event in the subject's life	I get a detailed understanding of this time in the subject's life

Send-Off *Today, when you work independently, find a picture book biography of the subject you are studying. Think about the information the author decided to write about and the structure the author used. Write your thoughts on a sticky note and be prepared to share when we gather as a group at the end of the workshop.*

Group Wrap-Up [Have students share the picture book biographies they are reading and explain the structure of the writing. Lead the class in a discussion of how understanding the structure of the writing helps us understand and organize the information.]

LESSON 9C

Using Article Structures to Help Us Understand Biography

Special Notes Use the internet to locate articles for student-selected subjects

Thinking Behind the Lesson Every biography format has specific structural features that help readers understand the text.

Materials Transparencies of biographical articles, varied subjects, that have different structures:

- an overview of someone's life
- a recounting of a particular event
- an analysis of a particular part of someone's life (Ben Franklin's inventions, for example)

Teacher provides one article for each student about the person he or she is studying (The Internet provides a rich source of articles; however, be attentive to the readability of text. It is preferable for the teacher to bookmark appropriate sites.)

Anchor chart: Structure of Biographies (from Lesson 9a)

Connection *We have been studying the structure of biographies as a way to help us understand and organize the information in them. We have learned that chapter book biographies are often chronological presentations of the important events in the subject's life. Picture books may also be chronological, with each page focusing on a different event, or they may focus on a single event.*

Explicit Instruction *Today, we are going to analyze the structure of biographical articles.* [Project the first article on the overhead.] *I will read this article aloud while you follow along silently. Concentrate on what the article is about and how the author organized the information.*

[Read the first section of the article aloud. Stop and think aloud about the information the author is sharing and the way it is organized. Here are some possibilities:

- summary of subject's life: important events in chronological order
- a recounting of one event in the subject's life
- an analysis of one aspect of the subject's life: his importance as an inventor, patriot, politician, etc.]

Hmmm. I can see that this article is about [subject's name]. The author tells us about ____. Now that I know the focus of the article and how the author structured the writing, I will have an easier time understanding and organizing the information.

Structure of Biographies

Type of Biography	Structure	How It Helps Me
Chapter book	Chronological presentation of important events	I know the order in which things happened I can easily identify important events I can create a time line
Picture book	Chronological presentation of important events; each page captures one event	I know the order in which things happened I can easily identify important events I can create a time line
Picture book	Description of one event in the subject's life	I get a detailed understanding of this time in the subject's life
Article	Summary of subject's life	I get an overview of the person's life and accomplishments
Article	Description of one important event	I get more in-depth information about a particular event
Article	Analysis of one aspect of subject's life	I get a better understanding of a particular aspect of person's life

Guided Practice *Let's look at another article together. Again, I'll read the first section aloud as you follow along silently. Think about the focus of the article and the way the author structured the writing.* [Read the first section of the second article aloud. Stop at a point where the students will have collected enough information to determine the focus of the article and the structure.]

Turn and talk with your partner. Discuss what the article is about and how the author structured the writing. Is the article a summary of the subject's life? Did the author select one event to write about? Did the author analyze one aspect of the person's life?

Send-Off *Today, I will provide you with an article about the subject of the biography you are reading. Read the first section and stop to think about the information the author is sharing and how it is structured. Does the article summarize the subject's life? Does the article focus on one event? Does the article analyze one aspect of the subject's life? Jot your thoughts down on a sticky note and continue to read the article to collect information.*

Group Wrap-Up *Let's share your findings about the articles you read. What were they about? How were they structured?* [Guide a class discussion.]

Strong readers use their understanding of text structure to help them understand and organize information.

LESSON 10

Understanding the Influence of Time and Place

Special Notes None

Thinking Behind the Lesson Understanding and discussing how the setting influences a subject's life is an opportunity to engage with the big ideas of text.

Materials Short biography of class subject

Connection *We've been studying biography—the history or story of a person's life. Fiction and biographies share many of the same literary elements.*

Explicit Instruction *The setting—time and place—is a particularly important element in a biography. The time and place in which a person lives affects his life.*

Readers think about what life was like when and where the subject was living. Very often, the setting (when and where) contributes to the obstacles that a person faces, so the accomplishments of the person are even more impressive.

A biography in which the setting is particularly important is that of Helen Keller. Helen Keller was born in 1880, nearly 130 years ago, in the southern state of Alabama. Life was very different then. They didn't have the medicines that we have today to help people when they became ill. They didn't have public education for all children. Despite these obstacles, Helen overcame severe handicaps to become a successful adult.

Guided Practice *Now, I'd like you to read a brief biography of the life of [subject's name]. While we're reading, think about the setting (time and place) in which this person lived. Use the questions below to scaffold discussion.*

- *How did the setting affect what happened to [subject's name]?*
- *How would his life have been different if he had been born today?*
- *Would the same obstacles be present today?*

Refer to the lessons in Unit 2, as needed, to scaffold discussion.

Send-Off *Today, while you are reading more of the biography you've chosen, think about how this person was affected by the setting (time and place) in which he or she lived.*

- *Did the time or place in which he or she lived provide particular obstacles the subject had to overcome to accomplish something?*
- *How might his or her life story have been different had it taken place during a different time period or in a different place?*
- *Do you think this person would still have an interesting biography if he or she had been born at a different time or place?*

Record your ideas in your reader's notebooks.

Group Wrap-Up [Have students share ideas about how settings influenced the lives of the people they are reading about.]

LESSON 11

Understanding the Influence of Other People

Special Notes None

Thinking Behind the Lesson Understanding how other people affect the subject of a biography is another opportunity to engage with the big ideas of text.

Materials Short biography of class subject

Three-column anchor chart: People Who Influenced the Biography Subject: Name and Relationship of Person/How He or She Influenced the Subject/My Thinking

One copy of anchor chart for each student (see template in Appendix L) to be glued in the reader's notebooks

Connection *The people we read about in biographies have overcome obstacles or accomplished something important. We have discussed how the time and place a person lives in can affect his or her life.*

Explicit Instruction *Today, we are going to talk about people in our subjects' lives who have influenced them positively or negatively. The dictionary defines influence as the capacity to get other people to do something or to think in a certain way. I am going to read a short biography about [subject's name] and think aloud about any people who may have influenced him.*

- *Who are the people who this subject admired?*
- *Who are the people who made the subject angry enough to act?*
- *Did anyone influence the subject in a negative way?*

[Read the first section of text. Stop at an appropriate spot to think aloud and record ideas on the "People Who Influenced the Biography Subject" chart.] *Hmmm. It says that [subject's name] decided [to do such and so] after he met [person's name] and [describe the experience]. I can infer that [subject's name] started to [describe a probable reaction] and did this. When someone influences another person, she convinces that person to think in a certain way.*

[Model, using your notes to articulate your thinking.]

Guided Practice *I am going to continue reading aloud as you follow along silently. As we read, make note of any people who have influenced [subject's name].* [Stop at an appropriate spot and lead students in a discussion of people who influenced the subject. Record their thinking on the three-column chart.]

- *Did this person have a positive or negative impact on [subject's name]?*
- *How did meeting this person change the subject's behavior, ideas, thinking?*

People Who Influenced the Biography Subject

Name and Relationship of Person	How He or She Influenced the Subject	My Thinking

Send-Off *Now you and a partner will read a short biography about [subject's name]. Look for people who influenced the subject in a positive or negative way. Record your thinking on your own three-column chart.*

[Alternatively:] *Today, during independent reading, think about people who influenced the subject of your biography. Record your thinking on your own three-column chart.*

Group Wrap-Up *Who found a person who helped the subject accomplish something or overcome an obstacle? Who encountered a person who hindered the subject's success? What does that make you think about?*

LESSON 12

Uncovering Character Traits

Special Notes None

Thinking Behind the Lesson Giving students the vocabulary to discuss a character makes their thinking go deeper and their oral language more precise.

Materials

Transparency of an example biography

One copy of a short biographical piece for each student (for partner work)

Three-column anchor chart: Uncovering Character Traits: Personality Trait/Evidence in Text and Page No./My Thinking

One copy of anchor chart for each student to be glued into reader's notebook

Connection

Fiction and biographies share many of the same literary elements. Characterization includes the things the author of the biography tells us about the subject that let us know what kind of person the subject is.

Explicit Instruction

Today, we are going to talk about how the subject of a biography is portrayed—his or her character traits. Is this person brave, hardworking, able to overcome adversity, determined? These are not physical characteristics that we can see. They are personality traits that are reflected in how people behave.

I am going to read an excerpt from this biography of [subject's name] and think aloud about his personality. I can make inferences about the subject's character from the words the author uses to describe him. I will also think about how the subject acts, what he says, and how other people react to him. I will record my thinking on the three-column chart.

Uncovering Character Traits

Personality Trait	Evidence in Text and Page No.	My Thinking

[Read aloud a portion of the biography in which the subject's character is revealed. Then share your thinking.] *OK, the author says [quote the author's words], and from that I infer that the subject is [character trait]. That makes me think . . .*

Guided Practice *Now we'll read some more of the biography. Follow along in your mind as I read aloud. At appropriate spots we'll stop and discuss what we have learned about the personality of this subject based on information in the text.*

[Read more of the text and stop at a point at which students will have gathered information to form an opinion about the personality traits of the subject.] *So how would you describe this character's personality? What evidence in the text makes you think that? How does this information influence your thinking?* [Record ideas on the three-column chart.]

[Continue to end of the text.]

Send-Off *When you are reading on your own, I want you to think about the person you are reading about. How would you describe the personality of this person? Record your thinking and evidence on your own three-column chart.*

Be prepared to share when we wrap up this workshop.

Group Wrap-Up [Have a few students share some character traits of their subjects and the supporting evidence.]

LESSON 13

Identifying Motivations That Cause People to Act

Special Notes None

Thinking Behind the Lesson Analyzing a biographical subject's motivations will enable students to uncover themes.

Materials A short biography about class subject

Three prepared sticky notes for each student: one labeled "Obstacles," one labeled "People," and one labeled "Events"

Four-column anchor chart: Probable Motivations: Subject/Obstacles/People/Events

Connection *We have discussed why authors choose to write about particular people.*

An author might write about someone who overcame obstacles, accomplished something important, or was the object of public fascination.

Explicit Instruction *When we read biographies, we gain a deeper insight into these people and become aware of the driving forces—the motivations—that led them to act, to bring about change. Driving forces may be obstacles that people need to overcome, people that influence them, or events to which they have no choice but to respond.*

Today, I'm going to read a biography about [subject's name]. This biography has lots of information, but I want to sift through it to find out exactly what motivated [subject's name] to be so successful in reaching her goal. So as I read, I'll be looking for

- *obstacles that might have created a problem*
- *people who might have been influential*
- *events that might have necessitated a response*

I'll put any information I find on sticky notes so I'll remember it.

[Begin to read the first chapter aloud, pausing to repeat a name, event, or obstacle that provides information about possible driving forces that motivated the subject to act. Record this information on a sticky note and place it on the four-column chart under the appropriate heading.]

Probable Motivations

Subject	Obstacles	People	Events

Guided Practice *Follow along as I finish reading the text aloud. I'm going to give you each three sticky notes, one headed "Obstacles," another headed "People," and a third headed "Events." If you find an obstacle, a person, or an event that was a driving force for this subject to act, jot it down on the appropriate sticky note. At the end we'll share our ideas and add our notes to the class chart.*

[When you finish reading, ask:] *So what are you thinking? What are your ideas about the driving forces that motivated the subject to act? Who would like to spark our discussion?* [Prompt discussion as needed.]

Look at our chart. We have discussed several driving forces that motivated this subject. Think about these ideas and find just the right words to develop a theory about the driving forces that motivated this subject to act. You might start like this: "There are several driving forces that caused [subject's name] to achieve the goal of ____." Turn and share with your partner and practice articulating your theory.

[Listen as partners share. Scaffold oral language as necessary to help students articulate or connect their ideas. Invite a few students to share their theories aloud, then arrive at a class theory.]

Send-Off *Look through the biography you are reading and identify driving forces—obstacles, people, and events—that motivated your subject to act. Record this information on the four-column chart.*

Group Wrap-Up [Have students share information about their subjects collected through their independent reading. (To keep information organized, have all students studying a particular subject share before moving on to a new subject.)]

Now that you have analyzed the driving forces that motivated your subject to act, ponder these ideas for a bit to find just the right words to articulate your theory. You might approach it like this:

Several driving forces motivated [subject's name] to act.
First . . .
Second . . .
Also . . .
Finally . . .
The result was . . .

[Optional: Provide the above paragraph frame for students who need extra support.]

LESSON 14

Developing Theories About How a Subject's Accomplishments Changed Society's Perceptions and Attitudes

Special Notes None

Thinking Behind the Lesson Biographies are particularly important because their subjects have important roles in the development of society and culture.

Materials The short biography used in the previous lesson

Four-column anchor chart: Contribution to Society or Culture: Subject/Obstacles/Accomplishments/Contribution

Connection *We know that authors write biographies about people who have accomplished great things. They have often overcome obstacles within the time and place in which they lived to achieve their goals.*

Explicit Instruction *More important, though, their struggle often changes our perceptions of what is possible. Let me show you what I mean. For example: In 1969, Golda Meir became the first female prime minister of Israel. Many people in the world at that time felt women weren't capable of being a leader of a country; they were supposed to be home raising families. Becoming the first woman prime minister of Israel was a big accomplishment in and of itself. But in doing so, Golda Meir also changed the perceptions of people worldwide about women being strong enough and smart enough to be world leaders. She became an important role model for young women.* Record this thinking on a four-column chart.]

Contribution to Society or Culture

Subject	Obstacles	Accomplishments	Contribution
Golda Meir	Being a woman in 1969	Became prime minister of Israel	Showed that women can lead countries; became a role model for young women worldwide

Guided Practice *Think about the subject of the biography you are reading. What obstacles did he or she face? What did he or she accomplish? How did his or her accomplishment help change a stereotype or a perception of society? Turn and share your initial thinking with your partner.*

Send-Off *Today, I want you to ponder this question: How did the accomplishments of your subject change society? Think about the obstacles he or she overcame and how the contribution he or she made changed the perceptions and views of society. Record your ideas on a four-column chart.*

When you are finished, quietly share your thinking with your partner. Once partners have had the opportunity to talk, we will regroup and discuss the themes you found.

[Listen to partnerships as they synthesize their ideas about how their subjects changed society's perceptions. Choose a few ideas to highlight during the wrap-up.]

Group Wrap-Up *Now that you are finished reading and rereading the text, what changes in the perception of society did your subject's struggle bring about?*

[Discuss various themes students infer about their subjects. Discuss how these broader effects on society make the subjects' accomplishments last throughout history.]

LESSON 15

Inferring Common Themes

Special Notes Use anchor charts from previous lessons for reference. Refer to Unit 2, Lesson 13 as needed to support partnership talk.

Thinking Behind the Lesson Synthesizing common themes uncovered during the biography unit creates a strong appreciation of the genre and its literary value.

Materials Familiar biography previously used in your instruction

Two-column anchor chart: Inferring Themes in Biographies/Evidence to Support Thinking

Inferring Themes in Biographies	Evidence to Support Thinking

Connection *We have been looking closely at the genre of biography. We know it is the story or history of a person's life. Reading biographies allows us to come to know people we wouldn't meet in our daily life. We have learned that a theme is the big idea or lesson about life that the author wants us to think about after we read.*

Guided Interaction *Today, we are going to take a closer look at themes that are common to many biographies. These include*

- *personality traits that are common to influential people*
- *types of events that trigger people to act*
- *relationships and support people need in order to act*

For example, many of the subjects of the biographies we have read believed in humanitarian rights. No matter how many times Martin Luther King Jr., Gandhi, and Nelson Mandela were told no, they kept fighting for what they believed in. Knowing this, I can say that if you hold strong beliefs about humanitarian rights, you can overcome obstacles that others put in your way.

Think about all the people we have studied over the course of our biography unit. [Refer to class charts from previous lessons.] *Turn and talk with your partner. What kinds of personality traits are common to many of the subjects we have studied?* [Listen and identify common ideas.]

One trait I heard you talking about is ____. Who had that idea? [Invite a student to start the discussion.] *Who can talk more about that?* [Invite students to share the evidence they are using to support their thinking.]

A second theory I heard is ____. Who wants to talk about that?

[Continue until discussion tapers off. Record final thinking on class chart.]

Send-Off *Today, during independent reading, you and your reading partner will think about the events that cause people to act. Think about all the various biographies we have read and the events we identified that caused people to act. Develop a theory about the kinds of events that cause people to take action. Use your reader's notebook to find evidence to support your thinking.*

Be prepared to share when we wrap up this workshop.

Group Wrap-Up *You and your partner have been discussing the types of events that cause people to act, and I want to hear what you are thinking. Remember to use the conversational moves and body language of strong speakers and listeners to help deepen our discussion. Who wants to start us off?* [Prompt students to include evidence to support their thinking.]

LESSON 16

Understanding How Reading Biography Affects You as a Person

Special Notes Refer to Unit 2, Lesson 17 Using Talking Points

Thinking Behind the Lesson Understanding that literature affects them is a powerful life lesson for students.

Materials The biographies students have read during the unit

All the graphic organizers students have filled in

Connection *We have been learning about and reading biographies for a month now. We have developed theories about the people, obstacles, and events that shape a person.*

Guided Interaction *Authors write biographies to introduce us to people we would not meet in our daily lives. They let us stand beside these people and experience their struggles and accomplishments. They also expect that reading about these extraordinary people will affect us as human beings and change how we live our lives.*

For example, reading about Golda Meir has shown me the kind of strength a woman can have in spite of societal views. Walking beside Golda has caused me to realize that a regular person like me can be strong and accomplish great things. Knowing this changes who I am and how I think and act.

In this unit we read a biography about [subject's name] together. We examined his accomplishments and the obstacles he overcame. [Review previously created class charts.] *How does this change you as a person and the way you will live your life? Turn and talk with your partner.* [Listen to the conversations and identify a few common ideas.]

One theory I heard is ____. Who had that idea? [Invite a student to start the discussion.] *Who can talk more about that?* [Invite students to share the evidence they are using to support their thinking.]

A second theory I heard is _____. Who would like to talk about that?

[Continue until discussion tapers off. Record final thinking on the class chart.]

Send-Off *While you are working on your own today, I want you to ponder how learning about your subject has affected you as a person. How has knowing about the obstacles and accomplishments of the subject changed how you think about people and the way you live your life? Use talking points to write down your ideas to share when we wrap up this workshop.*

Group Wrap-Up *How has meeting the influential person who was the subject of the biography you read affected you as a person and how you will live your life in the future? Who wants to start our discussion off?* [Scaffold oral language to help students articulate their thinking.]

UNIT 4

Author Study for Developing Analytical Readers

Although fourth graders have already been exposed to many authors in the previous grades, they are now expected to do more writing in more genres, and it is therefore important to develop their insight into and understanding of the different structures and techniques used by other writers. Katie Wood Ray, author of *Wondrous Words*, says: "In order to gather a repertoire of craft possibilities that will help a writer write well, that writer first has to learn how to read differently, how to read with a sense of possibility, a sense of 'What do I see here that might work for me in my writing?' This is what reading like a writer means—to read with a sense of possibility" (1999, 14).

We have based this unit of study on Ray's work. In it, students identify and name techniques used by a specific author (to evoke an emotional response or create a strong visual image, for example). Once having noticed and named these techniques, they apply them to their own writing.

Throughout this unit, you will be teaching students how to read, talk, think, and write about what they notice in the books they read. Reading several books by the same author, students begin to identify common themes and a characteristic style. Researching the author's life, they learn what compels the author to write the stories she or he does. They can then use this same lens to analyze the work of authors they encounter throughout their reading lives.

There are two ways to conduct an author study. In either case, the author being spotlighted must have written books at varied levels of difficulty so all students have access to text.

The first way is to select a single author to study as a class, using certain of her or his books during focus lessons and having students read additional books by this author during independent reading. You'll need to read a great many books by the author you choose, not just one or two, in order to become familiar with the span—and the possibilities—within his or her work. Fourth graders are ready for longer, more serious texts than those they have encountered in previous grades. However, we recommend that for this unit you choose an author who writes both picture books and chapter books. The readers in your classroom will have a range of abilities, and this way you can meet all their needs.

The second way is to use the work of a specific author during whole-class focus lessons and allow students to read another author of their choosing on their own. (You may want to have students who have chosen the same author work together in pairs or groups.) We emphasize that the modeling you do during the focus lessons should still spotlight the work of one author, since you'll be making connections between this author's books and identifying some of his or her common themes.

If you read one author as a class, you will need to assemble a great many copies of as many books by that author as you can find. If your students read different authors, you will need to assemble books by those authors after students have made their final choices. (Don't panic. Remember, your students can check books out from the school or local public library!) Remember that matching your students' ages and interests with an author's topics, social appropriateness, and readability goes a long way toward ensuring their motivation and engagement. You should also select authors whose writing you admire. You'll be spending a lot of time with their work, as will your students, so it had better be good. (Eve Bunting, Eloise Greenfield, Jerry Pinkney, Patricia Polacco, Cynthia Rylant, William Steig, Mildred Taylor, Chris Van Allsburg, and Jacqueline Woodson are just a few suggestions.)

Once again, the unit begins with immersion (Nia 1999). For the first two or three days, let students browse the work of a single author (whom you've chosen as a class or whom they've chosen individually) in order to become familiar with common characteristics and topics.

Next, invite students to begin reading books by this author, as well as thinking, talking, and writing about the author and his or her work. Students should read between six and ten picture books or between two and five chapter books. Whenever possible, encourage them to read some of each.

In your focus lessons, help them identify writing techniques the author uses, develop theories about how and why the author writes the stories he or she does, where the author gets ideas and inspiration, and how he or she takes snippets from real life and weaves them into the stories. Then, as they become familiar with the author's style, encourage them to attempt to use some of the same craft techniques in their own writing.

Use picture books during these focus lessons and interactive read-alouds. Although they typically have only thirty or so pages, they still contain complex characters, an accurate historical perspective, sophisticated themes and concepts, and interesting vocabulary. Because they are short, students can readily revisit them while reading on their own. They are an attainable model for students' own writing.

Conclude the unit with a celebration. If you have studied a single author as a class, you might try writing something that captures his or her style. If the class has studied many different authors, have students who have read the same author share their favorite books and talk about what they've learned from them.

Taking a close look at the work of a single author deepens our understanding of and interest in where writers get ideas and how what they put on the page often reveals something about who they are, what they know, and where they've been. These authors become our mentors and coaches as we commit our own stories to paper.

Lesson 1	Lesson 2	Lesson 3	Lesson 4
Connecting with an Author's Work	Learning About an Author	Learning More About an Author	Setting Expectations and Making Predictions
Lesson 5	**Lesson 6**	**Lesson 7**	**Lesson 8**
Browsing Books to Decide Whether You Want to Read Them	Immersing Yourself in One Author's Work	Learning More About an Author by Reading an Interview	Using the Internet to Find Out About an Author
Lesson 9	**Lesson 10**	**Lesson 11**	**Lesson 12**
Synthesizing Information and Developing Theories	Developing Theories About Where Authors Get Their Ideas	Looking for Chronological Patterns and Connections	Synthesizing Themes and Finding Patterns
Lesson 13a★	**Lesson 13b★**	**Lesson 14★**	**Lesson 15**
Noticing an Author's Ways with Words	Noticing an Author's Ways with Structure	Trying Out an Author's Writing Style and Technique	Recommending Authors to Others (Author celebration!)

★Lessons with an asterisk are intended to be repeated to develop deeper understandings.

FIGURE 13 Unit Trajectory

LESSON 1

Connecting with an Author's Work

Special Notes None

Thinking Behind the Lesson Connecting with a particular author's work helps us love reading and create our identity as a reader. Knowing what we like about a particular author's work allows us to recommend that author to others.

Materials A collection of books by one or two of your favorite authors

Connection *We have been studying the way strong readers think. They use different thinking strategies to make sense out of text. Strong readers also think about the authors they read. They don't just have favorite books; they also have favorite authors they know they love and can rely on. They have an organized way of thinking about these authors and their work.*

Explicit Instruction *When you read a book in a series and you like it, you know how to read the other books in the series and wait eagerly for the next one to be published?*

Strong readers find authors that they like, even love. They read a lot by that author and begin to analyze and make connections between the texts. They develop theories about that author: why the author chooses the topics and characters she writes about, why the author uses the voice he does. They read about the author in interviews and biographies. The author becomes someone they know well, like a friend.

When you study an author, you are making connections and inferences to understand the author better. When you know an author well, you develop your identity as a reader.

As I was looking through my books last night, I found several authors that I have fallen in love with and have studied. [Hold up a few books you have read by the same author. Talk about what you learned. Mention a second author whose work you want to read more of.]

Guided Practice *Think about authors that you have read or are reading now. Picture their stories in your mind. What do you notice about that author or what do you wonder about that author? Turn and talk to your partner about what you wonder or notice about a favorite author.*

[Listen to these conversations and then ask a few students to share. Discuss the authors and qualities that students favor. Reinforce how they are developing their identities and voices as strong readers.]

Send-Off *When you read independently today, look at the books you have in your bag. Think about their authors. Have you read another book by any of these authors? Do you have more than one book by the same author? Think about what draws you toward that author or type of book.*

Group Wrap-Up *I am curious whether some of you are drawn to particular authors. Did you find that you have more than one book by an author? Have you read more than one book by a particular author?*

[Have students turn and talk about their author choices, or have students jot in their reader's notebooks what they noticed about their author choices.]

LESSON 2

Learning About an Author

Special Notes None.

Thinking Behind the Lesson Introducing the class to a number of works by the same author gives everyone a set of shared experiences. Students develop a common vocabulary and rely on the same texts and author to make observations and develop theories.

Materials First book by the author whose works you are using as examples in your focus lessons (and whose works the class as a whole may also be reading)

Anchor chart: What I Learned About [Author's Name]/What I'm Thinking

What I Learned About [Author's Name]	What I'm Thinking

Connection *Yesterday we talked about how strong readers study authors they love. Today, we are going to begin an author study. The author I have selected for us to study together is [author's name]. I chose her because teacher friends of mine have told me how much they enjoy her writing. She has also been nominated for or won several children's book awards, so I think she must be a very good writer.*

Explicit Instruction *Before I begin reading this book of hers, I'm going to examine the cover to learn as much about her and her writing as I can. That will help me understand where this author and the story are coming from.*

[Read the front and back covers or dust jacket. Discuss any biographical information. Discuss the kind of information that the publisher shares with the reader.]

Guided Practice [Have the students help you paraphrase information learned about the author as you record it on the anchor chart.]

[Read the book aloud, stopping at key points to discuss different ideas. Then discuss any questions or comments students have, anything they noticed or liked.]

Send-Off *When you read on your own today, don't forget to read the dust jacket or back cover to learn more about the author. Learning about the author helps you understand where the story is coming from.*

Group Wrap-Up [Have one or two students share something interesting they noted about the authors they are reading.]

LESSON 3

Learning More About an Author

Special Notes None

Thinking Behind the Lesson Reading several books by the same author allows us to gather evidence on which to base theories about that author and his or her work. We are able to discuss common themes, familiar characters, and particular situations.

Materials A second book by the spotlighted author

Anchor chart: What I Learned About [Author's Name]/What I'm Thinking (from Lesson 2)

Class chart: Synthesis Grid for Author Study (poster size) (see Appendix C)

One copy of the synthesis grid (enlarged to eleven by seventeen inches) for each student

Connection *Yesterday we began our study of [author's name]. We read [story title] and learned a few things about the author.* [Refer to anchor chart.]

Explicit Instruction *Today, I have a new book to share with you called [title]. Before I begin reading, I am going to examine the cover to see whether I can learn some more about this author.* [Read the back cover or dust jacket. Discuss any biographical information. Record new biographical information on the anchor chart.]

[Read the text aloud, stopping at key points to discuss different ideas. After you finish, discuss any questions, comments, or concerns.]

Now that we've read two books by the same author, we're starting to find out more information. We're going to collect this information on something called a synthesis grid so we'll be able to remember it and compare the information we learn from different sources.

[On the class chart, fill in the information learned from reading the first book and have students enter it on their copies. Explain how the class will collect information as you read each new book.]

Guided Practice [Have students help you add the information learned from reading the second book to the synthesis grid and enter it on their copies.]

[Have the students use the grid to make comparisons and form theories about this author. Ask them to turn and tell something to their partners that they noticed about both books. Scaffold talking in complete sentences:

- *I noticed in both books that* _____.
- *This makes me think that* _____.
- *I think that this author likes to* _____.
- *I think this because* _____.]

Send-Off *Today, when you read on your own, use what you know about the author to help you think more deeply about the story.*

Group Wrap-Up [Have one or two students share something interesting they noted about the authors they are reading.]

LESSON 4

Setting Expectations and Making Predictions

Special Notes None

Thinking Behind the Lesson Knowing something about an author enables us to make predictions about a book we are about to read. For example, if we know that an author tends to tell stories about people in her family, we might predict that the story we are about to read is going to be another family story or adventure.

Materials A third book by the spotlighted author

Anchor chart: What I Learned About [Author's Name]/What I'm Thinking (from Lesson 2)

Class chart: Synthesis Grid for Author Study (see Appendix C)

Students' individual copies of the synthesis grid

Connection *We have been studying [author's name]. We have read two stories by this author and have read some biographical information. We have been building our background knowledge about this author.*

Explicit Instruction *We can use this growing background knowledge to make predictions about and set expectations for this author's writing. Here is a third book by our author; it's called [title]. Look at the cover. I will read the back cover [dust jacket] to see whether it includes any biographical information we don't already know.* [Add new information to the anchor chart.]

Based on what I already know about this author, I predict ____. [Name one thing you expect to find in this new text.]

When I think about what I already know about an author before I start reading one of her books, it helps me prepare. I already start to think of the kind of story this author writes and the kind of language she uses.

Guided Practice *Think about what you have learned about this author so far. Turn and tell your partner one or two things you predict will be in this new book.* [Listen as students share some of their expectations.]

[Begin reading the book aloud, stopping at key points to allow students to make predictions. Scaffold their talk to connect their predictions to their background knowledge: *This character is like the character from the story* ____. Also note craft characteristics: *The illustrations in this book look like* ____.]

[Help students complete the synthesis grid for book 3.]

Send-Off *When you read on your own today, think about the background you already know about the book or author you are reading. Reflect on how knowing something about the author prepares you for reading.*

Group Wrap-Up [Have students share how their background knowledge helped prepare them for reading today.]

LESSON 5

Browsing Books to Decide Whether You Want to Read Them

Special Notes Students select the author whose work they will read, unless the whole class is reading books by the author you've chosen.

Thinking Behind the Lesson Readers have preferences and decide what to read based on personal taste.

Materials Collections of three to five books by seven to ten authors at readability levels appropriate for the class

One copy of selection sheet for each student: Author/What I Notice/What I Wonder

Author	What I Notice	What I Wonder

Connection *We have been studying [author's name]. We have collectively been increasing the background information we know about her. We have learned how we can make connections between an author's life and the books she writes.*

[Use the anchor charts the class has created to show students how they now read like the kind of reader who

- notices the ways of an author
- makes connections among texts
- understands how an author's life impacts his or her writing
- can synthesize information and develop theories about authors]

Explicit Instruction

[Explain that now, in pairs or groups, the students are going to choose authors to study.] *Today, you are going to browse the work of several authors and identify two or three authors you might like to study.*

[Model how you might decide which author to choose.]

- *This is a collection of books by [author's name]. I read [title] by her and really love that story. Maybe I would like other books she has written.*
- *These illustrations are amazing. I just love a book with ____.*
- *I have always heard about [author's name]. People think he is ____.*

Guided Practice

[Select another collection of books by a single author. Share the covers with students. Have students share anything they know about that author or why they think that he or she might be interesting to study.]

Send-Off

Today you are going to browse books by a number of authors. Be sure to look through each author's work. Notice the kind of topics the author writes about and the genre he or she writes in. Look at the illustrations. Read a bit and see whether you like the author's style.

On your recording sheet, indicate your first, second, and third choices, along with two things you notice or wonder about each.

Group Wrap-Up

[Have students share what they notice or wonder about the authors they browsed today.]

Before the next session, assign students to one of their choices. Be sure that author has a range of texts the students can access.

LESSON 6

Immersing Yourself in One Author's Work

Special Notes Selected author has been assigned (see Lesson 5)

Thinking Behind the Lesson When we read books by the same author, we begin to learn about that author. Each time we read a book, we gather more information about that author, his style, her topic choice.

Materials Collection of books by the author you're spotlighting

Collections of books by student-selected authors

Before the Lesson Assign authors to partnerships or groups based on interest and reading ability.

Connection *We have been learning about [author's name] together. Yesterday you browsed collections of books by different authors and made a short list of those you would like to study. I used your choices to form author study groups.* [Share author assignments.]

Explicit Instruction *When we first began reading and learning about our class author, we immersed ourselves in her writing by reading several of her books. We noticed things about the writing. We read the back covers or dust jackets to learn about the author's life. We talked about our thinking with others to form opinions.*

Today, you will begin to immerse yourselves in the work of one of the authors you told me were your top three choices.

Guided Practice *Sit together in your author study groups. Share why you selected that author. Share what you already know about the author. Read the back covers or dust jackets of the books. Discuss what these say about the author. In your reader's notebook, record what you have learned.*

Send-Off *Now you are going to go off on your own and begin to immerse yourself in the author's writing. Enjoy the stories and take note of anything you notice about the author's writing. Be prepared to share your thinking when we regroup at the end of the workshop.*

Group Wrap-Up [Have students share with their group what they noticed about the author. Listen to these conversations and take note of interesting thinking. Scaffold the discussions as needed.]

LESSON 7

Learning More About an Author by Reading an Interview

Special Notes Interviews can be found on the internet

Thinking Behind the Lesson By researching authors' backgrounds, we find out how they choose topics to write about and how they craft their writing.

Materials One copy of an interview with the author you're spotlighting for each student

A transparency of the interview (optional)

Anchor chart: What I Learned About [Author's Name]/What I'm Thinking (from Lesson 2)

Copies of interviews with the authors students are studying

Connection *We have been gathering information about the authors we are studying by reading the back covers and dust jackets of their books. Authors also give interviews to magazines and book publishers. An interview will give us a lot more information. The person asking questions often asks the same questions we would ask the author.*

Explicit Instruction *I've made copies of an interview with the author we are studying together as a class.* [Hand out copies and/or project the transparency. Explain how to read an interview if students haven't encountered one before.]

We will read a bit of the interview together and stop to think about any new information we learn about the author. [Read the first question and answer, then paraphrase: *Oh, I learned . . .* Decide whether it should be added to the anchor chart.]

Guided Practice [Read the next question and answer. Guide students as they paraphrase what they learned. Have partners read a section together, decide how to paraphrase it, and share it with the class. Record relevant information on the anchor chart.]

Send-Off

When you are working on your own today, start collecting information about the author you have chosen by reading the interview I've given you a copy of and the back covers or dust jackets of the books you have by this author. In your reader's notebook, set up a two-column chart with the headings "What I Learned About [Author's Name]" and "What I Am Thinking," and record any biographical information you learn.

Group Wrap-Up [Have partners and groups share the information they've learned about their author.]

LESSON 8

Using the Internet to Find Out About an Author

Special Notes None

Thinking Behind the Lesson The Internet is another tool we can use to research an author.

Materials Computer(s) with an Internet connection, with bookmarked (and school-approved) sources of author information

Anchor chart: What I Learned About [Author's Name]/What I'm Thinking (from Lesson 2)

Chart-size version of the Internet Research Grid for Author Study (see Appendix D), as well as a standard-size copy for each student

Connection *We know that by learning about an author, we can make connections between the author's life and his or her writing. Yesterday we read an interview with an author. We have also learned about authors from the back covers and dust jackets of their books. We can also do research in magazines, biographies, and memoirs and on the Internet.*

Explicit Instruction *Today, we are going to use the Internet to research background information about our class author and your individual authors.*

[Model using the Internet to research the author you are spotlighting in this unit. Take notes on the chart version of the synthesis grid, thinking aloud as you jot down a few key words to help you remember her books, awards and medals; biographical information; how she became an author; and any other interesting information.]

Guided Practice [After modeling with one or two websites, invite students to consult a website with a partner and select a few key words to note on the synthesis grid. Repeat as necessary until students are comfortable with the process.]

Send-Off *Today, you and your partner or group will have the opportunity to use the Internet to find and share information about the author you are studying.*

[Hand out additional copies of the synthesis grid if needed. Guide students in finding websites containing information about their authors and paraphrasing it on the grid.]

Group Wrap-Up [Have partners and teams share interesting information about their authors with the class and connect that information with the books the authors have written.]

LESSON 9

Synthesizing Information and Developing Theories

Special Notes None

Thinking Behind the Lesson Reading several books and consulting websites, interviews, and other biographical and critical sources provides rich information and insight into an author and his or her body of work.

Materials Three previously read books by the author you are spotlighting

Class synthesis grid (from Lesson 3)

Anchor chart: Developing Theories About [Author's Name]/Synthesizing My Thinking

Developing Theories About [Author's Name]	Synthesizing My Thinking

Connection *We have been learning background knowledge about [author's name] and collecting information about her life and her books on our synthesis grid.*

Explicit Instruction *Strong readers think about all they know about an author's writing and the author's life and connect this information to develop theories about the author and his or her work. In a way it's like connecting a series of dots to form a complete image. This is called* synthesis. *When we synthesize our thinking, we connect information and develop a theory—we think about the whole picture.*

For example, when I look at our synthesis grid, I can see that [author's name] used ____ in all three of her books. I have developed a theory that this author likes to ____. I haven't read that anywhere, but it seems that if she ____, then my theory is logical. [Enter the theory on the anchor chart "Developing Theories About [Author's Name]/Synthesizing My Thinking."]

Do you see how synthesis works? I use the bits of information that I have gathered, find the connections, and develop a theory. I synthesize my thinking.

Guided Practice [Guide students in using the class synthesis chart to develop a theory about another aspect of this author.] *Look at what we wrote down for ____. Think about the connections between those texts. What theory can we develop from that?* [Add to anchor chart.] *See how you connected pieces of information and developed a theory—some new thinking.*

Look at the class synthesis grid. Reread the information we have collected. See if you can make any connections to develop a theory about this author. Turn and talk about it with your partner. Remember, if you can say it then you can write it. [Model writing the class theory on an overhead or chart paper.]

Send-Off *You have been reading a lot by and about your author. Today when you are working on your own, think about all you have learned about the author. Review your synthesis grid. Connect some of the information you have learned, and synthesize your thinking about your author. See whether you can develop a theory about this author's writing.*

Group Wrap-Up [Have a few students share theories they have developed about their authors. Prompt them to explain the evidence they synthesized to develop their theories.]

Now that you have articulated your theories with your partner, write your thinking in your reader's notebook.

LESSON 10

Developing Theories About Where Authors Get Their Ideas

Special Notes None

Thinking Behind the Lesson Knowing something about an author helps us theorize where authors get their ideas.

Materials

Texts read so far by and about the author you are spotlighting, displayed so students can see covers

Anchor chart: What I Learned About [Author's Name]/What I'm Thinking (from Lesson 2)

Class Synthesis Grid for Author Study (from Lesson 3)

Anchor chart: Developing Theories About [Author's Name]/Synthesizing My Thinking (from Lesson 9)

Connection

We have been reading and learning about [author's name]. We have synthesized information and developed theories about this author.

From your own writing, you know that authors write about what they know and care about. We can use what we already know about the author to develop theories about where the author gets the ideas for her stories.

Explicit Instruction

Today, we are going to examine the evidence we have collected and develop theories about why [author's name] wrote the type of stories she did. We will record these theories on an anchor chart.

[Use the information on the synthesis grid to model how you use evidence to develop a theory.] *We learned from reading interviews and articles that . . . We can see in [book title] and [book title] that . . . I can make the connection that this author took something from her own life to write about ____. My theory is ____.*

Guided Practice *Look at all the texts we have read so far by and about [author's name]. Think about what you know about her. Turn and talk with your partner about any other theories you have about where she gets ideas for her writing.*

[Listen as partners discuss theories. Share some of their thinking.

Add these ideas to the anchor chart "Developing Theories About [Author's Name]/ Synthesizing My Thinking." Discuss whether there are any common topics or themes across the texts. Are there any texts that don't fit the pattern?]

Send-Off *When you are working with your partner or group today, think about the author you are studying. Think about what you know about the author's life and what you notice in his or her writing.*

Discuss possible theories of where this author gets ideas for his or her writing. Record your theories in your reader's notebook.

Group Wrap-Up [Have pairs or groups share their theories about where the authors they are studying got their ideas. What is the evidence for their theories? Did they read an interview? Did they notice patterns of topics or themes across the set of texts?]

LESSON 11

Looking for Chronological Patterns and Connections

Special Notes None

Thinking Behind the Lesson Examining an author's work in the order it was written provides a historical time line of his or her evolution as a writer.

Materials All the texts the class has read by the author you are spotlighting

Class Synthesis Grid (from Lesson 3)

Anchor chart: Developing Theories About [Author's Name]/Synthesizing My Thinking (from Lesson 9)

Connection *We have read many books by [author's name] and developed theories about her as an author.*

Explicit Instruction *The copyright date of a book is the year in which it was published; it's the book's "birthday." If we order [author's] books by their copyright dates, we may find patterns and connections or see an evolution to [author's] writing.*

The first book we read was [title]. The copyright date of that book is ____. [Record the date on the class synthesis grid.] *The second book we read was [title]. This book came before [after] the first book we read.* [Add the date to the class synthesis grid.]

[Begin to arrange the books by order on the ledge of the whiteboard or in some other prominently visible place.]

Guided Practice [Hand out other texts to pairs or groups. Have them locate the copyright dates and place the books in chronological order. Add the dates to the class synthesis grid.]

[Discuss patterns and connections and form theories about the evolution of the author's writing. Discuss any events in the author's life that may have impacted her writing. Record the theories the class develops on the anchor chart.]

Send-Off

When you are working independently with your partner or group, take some time to put the books you've read in chronological order. Discuss any connections to the author's life and writing and develop theories about the evolution of the author's writing. Record your ideas in your reader's notebook. Be prepared to share at Group Wrap Up.

Group Wrap-Up

What did you notice about your author today? Did you develop any theories of how your author's writing evolved over time? Did anything from the author's life have an impact on his or her writing?

LESSON 12

Synthesizing Themes and Finding Patterns

Special Notes None

Thinking Behind the Lesson After reading several books by one author, we are able to synthesize themes.

Materials All the books the class has read by the author you are spotlighting

Anchor chart: Developing Theories About [Author's Name]/Synthesizing My Thinking (from Lesson 9)

Class Synthesis Grid (from Lesson 3)

Two-column anchor chart: Possible Theme/My Thinking

Connection *We have been reading and thinking about books written by [author's name]. We have made connections among these texts and have developed theories about the author.*

Explicit Instruction *Today we are going to discuss the theme of [author's] books. The theme is an important idea about people, life, or society that the author wants to share. It is an idea about life the author wants us to think about, to ponder for a while.*

One of the stories by [author's name] that we read is [title]. The story is about [retell/summarize the plot], but the important idea about life—the theme—that the author wants me to think about is ____. [Write the theme on the new two-column anchor chart.]

The author doesn't come right out and tell me the theme. I have to make inferences—connect clues or evidence—from the text to synthesize the theme. [Flip through the text and think aloud how the events in the story helped you synthesize the theme: *This part when ____, and then ____ made me think about ____.* Add this thinking to the chart.]

Guided Practice [Select a second book by this author. Guide the class to summarize the story.]

All right, that was what happened in the story. Now think about why the author wrote the story. What is the important idea about life that the author is trying to tell us? [Record possible themes on the two-column chart.]

[Prompt students to discuss the thinking that led them to these themes. Record their thinking on the chart.]

Send-Off

On your own, reread a book by the author you are studying. Think about the theme, the important idea about people, life, or society in the story. What important idea does the author want you to think about? What evidence from the text makes you think that is the theme? Record the theme and your thinking in your reader's notebook. Be prepared to share your thoughts when we come together at the end of readers' workshop.

Group Wrap-Up

[Select a few students to share the themes they synthesized from the books they have read.]

LESSON 13A

Noticing an Author's Craft: Ways with Words

Special Notes Refer to: Ray, Katie Wood. 1999. *Wondrous Words: Writers and Writing in the Elementary Classroom*. Urbana, IL: NCTE.

Thinking Behind the Lesson Identifying and naming an author's writing techniques allows readers to analyze these techniques and apply them to their own writing.

Materials All the books the class has read by the author you are spotlighting

Copies of typed excerpts from two of the stories for each student

Transparencies of these excerpts (optional)

Anchor chart: Author's Craft

Connection *People learn to talk from the people around them. You sound like your parents. If you have relatives who live in other parts of the country, they might have a different accent and their kids will talk like them.*

Explicit Instruction *The same is true of writers. Writers write like the people they love to read. Writers hear echoes of their favorite authors in their heads. They know these authors so well, they can hear their voices. Here's what Katie Wood Ray, on page 71 of her 1999 book* Wondrous Words, *says about voice: "Voice is made up of rhythms, intonations, pitches, and ways with words. In written voice, punctuation, sentence structure, and word selection give the writing its sound, its voice. And that sound is a learned thing. We sound like the sounds we have heard before. If we immerse ourselves in new sounds, before long we can make those sounds our own."*

When I want to really look at how an author uses words in his or her writing, I read a piece over and over. I notice the words being used, how they are punctuated. I think about how the author is telling the story. This helps me to find the sound, the rhythm—the voice.

[Hand out copies of the first excerpt. Read it aloud a few times and think aloud how you identify the voice.] *When I think about [author's] ways with words, I notice it sounds like she is _____. I am going to enter this on the chart.* [Do so.]

Author's Craft

Title:

Author:

Genre:

	Notice	Example	Why did the author do this?
Ways with Words	Striking Verbs that Evoke Emotions		
Ways with Structures			

Guided Practice [Have students read the next excerpt silently a few times. Remind them to think about the words, the punctuation, and how the author is telling the story. Then reread the excerpt chorally as a class and have students identify additional aspects of the author's way with words. Enter them on the chart.]

Send-Off *Here are copies of more of [author's] books. During independent reading, read and reread the book you've been given. Notice how [author's name] uses words and punctuation. Think about how she is telling the story. Hear the sound, the voice of the writing.*

Group Wrap-Up [Have several students read a passage aloud and share their thoughts about the voice they hear. What ways with words give it that sound?]

LESSON 13B

Noticing an Author's Ways with Structure

Special Notes Refer to: Ray, Katie Wood. 1999. *Wondrous Words: Writers and Writing in the Elementary Classroom*. Urbana, IL: NCTE.

Thinking Behind the Lesson Identifying and naming an author's writing techniques allows readers to analyze these techniques and apply them to their own writing.

Materials All the books the class has read by the author you are spotlighting

Copies of typed excerpts from two of these stories for each student (Pick passages that contain examples of structural techniques.)

Transparencies of these excerpts (optional)

Anchor chart: Author's Craft (from Lesson 13a)

Connection *Yesterday we talked about how we sound like the people we live with and listen to. We discussed the idea that authors develop their writing voice by emulating the punctuation, sentence structure, and word selection of the writers they read a lot.*

Explicit Instruction *Today, we are going to look more deeply at reading like a writer. We are going to locate places where it looks like the author is deliberately doing something with language structure.*

[Hand out copies of the first excerpt. Show students the structural technique. Name it. Write down the example on the anchor chart.

Develop a theory about why the author used that technique. How does it affect the writing? Record your thinking on the three-column chart.]

Author's Craft

Title:

Author:

Genre:

	Notice	Example	Why did the author do this?
Ways with Words	Striking Verbs that Evoke Emotions		
Ways with Structures	Flashbacks Slowing Down Time		

Guided Practice [Hand out copies of the second excerpt. Have students read the passage with a partner. Have them find a structural technique the author has used, name it, and think about why the author may have done that. Enter it on the Author's Craft anchor chart.]

Send-Off *On your own, read a short piece of text by the author you are studying. Reread it like a writer and see whether you can find places where it seems like the author is doing something deliberately with structure. Set up a three-column chart in your reader's notebook and record your thinking.*

Group Wrap-Up [Have two or three students share passages in which their authors used a deliberate crafting technique.]

LESSON 14

Trying Out an Author's Writing Style and Technique

Special Notes None

Thinking Behind the Lesson Once we have identified and named writing techniques, we can apply them to our own writing.

Materials Anchor chart: Author's Craft (from Lesson 13a)

A piece of your own writing, on a chart or transparency

Connection *We have been reading like a writer and noticing an author's ways with words and structure. We have been thinking about why authors choose to use particular techniques and the effects the techniques have on their writing.* [Review the two-column chart the class has been creating.]

Explicit Instruction *Readers learn from authors and try those techniques in their own writing. One technique [author's name] uses is ____. I am going to show you how I can look back in my own writing and try out that technique.*

[On the chart or transparency of your own writing, identify a spot where you could try the author's technique. Make the appropriate revision.]

Do you see how I can purposely use something I learned from the author to make my writing better?

Guided Practice *Pick a piece of writing in your writer's notebook. Reread it and find a spot where you can try out this technique. Does it sound better? Does it work in your writing?*

Send-Off *Today, I want you to work on a piece of writing in your writer's notebook. (You can write something new instead if you wish.) Try some of the writing techniques our class author uses in her writing. Add these techniques to your own writing toolbox.*

Group Wrap-Up [Have two or three students share passages in which they used a particular technique. Discuss how writers are purposeful in using these tools.]

Now that you know these techniques exist, you can use them to make your own writing stronger.

LESSON 15

Recommending Authors to Others

Special Notes None

Thinking Behind the Lesson Sharing books, ideas, and passions builds a reading community.

Materials Collections of books by the author you spotlighted in the unit and by the authors students chose to focus on

A paragraph frame to scaffold language in talking about authors (optional)

Connection *We have been immersing ourselves in the work of [author's name] and identifying what we liked about her books.*

Explicit Instruction *When I read books by an author I like, I want to share them with my friends who also love to read. I explain a bit about the books and why I like them. I share information about the type of writing the author does, the plots, the characters, his or her ways with words. I share interesting things I know about the author's life and how that connects to the books.*

For example, I have been sharing information about [name of the author you are spotlighting] with the other fourth-grade teachers. I told them [fill in the appropriate details]. Now they want to use her books in their classrooms!

Guided Practice *Turn to your partner [group]. Think about all you know about the author you have been studying. What are some things you want to share with other readers? What exciting things about this author do you want to share with your friends to get them interested in reading his or her books?*

Send-Off *With your partner [group], decide what information about your author you will use to recommend him or her to your classmates. Create a poster highlighting this author's work and the reasons you are recommending him or her.*

Group Wrap-Up [Have students celebrate their authors by displaying their books. Ask each pair or group to give a brief presentation recommending its author. The book displays and posters can be left up for a week or two to entice students to read books from a new author who intrigues them.]

Closing Thoughts

Designing Your Own Units of Study

This book includes units of study on Reading Tools for Developing Active Readers, Discussion Skills for Developing Thoughtful Readers, Genre Study for Developing Sophisticated Nonfiction Readers, and an Author Study for Developing Analytical Readers. Now it's your turn to develop your own units of study on specific topics, genres, and concepts that need to be taught in your school or district.

Identify a Year's Worth of Units of Study

There are approximately eight unit-length chunks of time in a school year. Depending on its goals and scope, a unit takes between three and six weeks to present. Setting start and end dates promotes rigorous instruction and keeps you from lingering or going off on tangents. However, until you and your students become familiar with the format, units of study may take more time than your current pedagogical approach. Remember to take the time you and your students need; don't rush through the content simply because the allotted time is running out. This is not "surfboard teaching"—skimming the surface of a topic and moving on to the next. The overall goal is to develop a deep understanding and mastery of the concepts.

A literacy unit of study may focus on a comprehension strategy, a genre, an author, or a line of inquiry. Sometimes you can design a unit that addresses two goals simultaneously. For example, if a unit focuses on a single comprehension strategy, such as making connections, building it around an author study will encourage deeper discussions. A list of possible units of study is provided in Figure 14.

- Launching a Readers' Workshop
- Using Reading Strategies to Figure Out Words
- Thinking and Talking About Books
- Using Comprehension Strategies
- Reading Like a Writer
- Investigating Characters
- Conducting Nonfiction Research
- Exploring Structure
- Identifying and Using Test-Taking Strategies
- Developing Fluency
- Studying an Author
- Studying a Genre (folktales, fairy tales, fables, mysteries, historical fiction, fantasy, poetry, biography/autobiography, memoir, essays and articles)
- Exploring New Authors
- Exploring New Genres
- Strengthening a Particular Skill, Behavior, or Strategy

FIGURE 14 Possible Units of Study for a Readers' Workshop

Designing your yearlong curriculum is a challenging process that warrants collaboration and collegiality. Begin by reviewing lists of the units your colleagues typically teach. Pay particular attention to the topics that are taught in previous grades so you can build on them and at the same time avoid repetition. Knowing who does what, and when and why they do it, helps you develop better, more fluent readers and extend and deepen your students' learning. Be aware of state and local standards for fourth grade and whether standardized tests will be administered. Looking over your list, keep an eye out for literacy content (genres, comprehension strategies) versus topical content (astronomy, pollution, Colonial times).

Balancing knowledge, content, and instruction is key. A good mix includes one author study, one genre study, two nonfiction studies tied to content studies and self-selected research, perhaps one or two comprehension studies, a craft study, a test-taking unit, and one or two units directed toward a particular class' interests and needs (one sample calendar is shown in Figure 15). As you determine the order in which to present the units, think about their purpose and how they connect with one another and with your existing curriculum. Writing the name of each unit on a sticky note lets you move

Month	Unit of Study	Focus Lesson Topics
September	Being Present in Your Reading: Using Active Reading Strategies	• Being present in your reading, listening to your thinking • Creating images in your mind • Using background knowledge • Making inferences • Merging strategies • Using tools to hold on to thinking
October/ November	Becoming Thoughtful Readers, Speakers, and Thinkers	• Talking to one another around the circle • Developing theories about characters, situations, themes • Using conversational moves and body language • Disagreeing respectfully • Using evidence to support thinking
November/ December	Studying Biography	• Defining biographies • Identifying characteristics of the genre • Analyzing why authors write about certain subjects • Sifting important events, details, interesting information
December/ January	Poetry	• Identifying characteristics of poetry • Developing fluency using white space, line breaks, font, and punctuation • Identifying and using literary devices to get inside poetry • Identifying themes • Savoring language: word choice
January	Studying Other Nonfiction	• Setting a purpose for reading • Reading nonfiction with active reading strategies • Using text features to read efficiently • Sifting main ideas and details • Synthesizing information • Articulating knowledge orally and in writing
February	Taking Tests	• Identifying characteristics • Learning the traps • Carefully reading and understanding questions • Using active reading strategies to read unfamiliar or difficult material • Recognizing what the question is asking

FIGURE 15 Sample Fourth-Grade Unit-of-Study Planning Calendar

Month	Unit of Study	Focus Lesson Topics
March	Studying an Author	• Connecting with the author's work • Researching the author's life to understand his or her characters and stories • Finding patterns in the author's work • Reading like a writer to analyze the author's craft • Trying the author's moves in your own writing
April	Studying Craft	• Using words to create sensory images • Using strong verbs • Developing leads and endings • Recognizing things to avoid (too many adjectives, redundancies, common words) • Using specific words and names
May–June	Choices appropriate to the students and the circumstances	

FIGURE 15 *Continued*

them around easily on your planning calendar. (A template for mapping out your units of study is provide in Appendix M.)

Base comprehension studies on your students. Many schools teach comprehension strategies beginning in kindergarten. Your fourth graders will probably know how to make connections or create sensory images, but they may not be using those strategies flexibly and concurrently. Or they may not be comfortable articulating their ideas and writing them down. In schools where explicit instruction in comprehension is a new idea, students benefit from units that go deeper into individual strategies, allowing them to own each one. Unit 1, "Reading Tools for Developing Active Readers" shows students how to merge key strategies in order to be present in their reading. For more information on units devoted to a particular comprehension strategy, see Keene and Zimmermann's *Mosaic of Thought* (2007) and Harvey and Goudvis' *Strategies That Work* (2007) or *The Comprehension Toolkit* (2005).

Our biography unit shows students how to read nonfiction using the same active strategies they use when reading fiction. The unit doesn't teach one biography; it teaches strong reader strategies and literary concepts using biography to ground this reading work. The lessons in this unit on developing theories by accumulating evidence are at the heart of reading nonfiction. You can use the biography unit as a template for units that explore the characteristics of other nonfiction texts.

Do Your Research

Once you have selected your units of study, read, read, read. What do the experts say about the comprehension strategy, the genre, the craft? Learn what you need to know in order to be able to make the invisible moves of strong readers and speakers visible, to unlock the mystery of the genre, and to name and teach the elements of an author's craft. The odd thing is, the more knowledge you have, the simpler and more concrete your language becomes. You'll use fewer words and more precise language to define and teach something you know well. While researching the topic, create a list of possible focus lessons. Also consult the state and district standards to ensure your students will meet them.

Plan the Trajectory

A unit of study progresses from concrete introductory focus lessons to complex focus lessons dealing with analysis and synthesis. Write the topic of each lesson on a sticky note and juggle the order until you have a trajectory that makes sense. (A template for planning a monthlong unit trajectory is provided in Appendix N.)

Write the Focus Lessons

You may find that first talking the lessons out with a partner will speed things along. Recognize too that it is difficult to explain invisible processes. Writing the lessons is like working with clay. As they begin to take form, you can knead them into ever more refined renditions. Envision your students in front of you: how they will respond. The key is to find a simple sentence or two that explains the strategy, technique, or characteristic so that fourth graders will understand. Use their language: *an inference is probably true.* Start talking or writing, and you will find just the right words to make your teaching explicit.

Writing out each lesson is particularly useful when you are getting started. It is the only way to sharpen your language. Following a template allows you to separate teaching the strategy or concept from teaching the text. The text is the vehicle through which students will grow stronger literacy skills they can then use with other texts not tied to the unit. (Blank Focus Lesson Planning Sheet templates are provided in Appendices O and P.)

Materials

Finding the right texts is critical. They must highlight the concept you are teaching and match the readability levels of all students in the class so that everyone can read and practice what is taught. Exposing students to quality literature will help them develop a deeper understanding of literacy and give them the best possible model for developing their own.

Connection

Base your connections on the work students have done previously. (You can do this even in the first lesson of a new unit.) Remind students that what they are learning today is connected to what they did yesterday, or in the previous unit, or last year. This connection eases their way: *We have been studying how to do so and so. We already know that we can thus and such.* Students become aware that their knowledge is becoming more sophisticated, that they are expected to carry their prior learning along with them. They begin to see that the acquisition of skills and knowledge is not an isolated activity.

Explicit Instruction

Write down what you will say and do. Don't simply write a list of directions: *define, read a bit, think aloud, turn and talk, share.* Until you write down the words you will use to explain the strategy or concept, your language will not be concrete and concise. Teachers who wing it, who extemporize with their students in front of them, flounder, and their lessons are unclear. Writing out your instruction helps you find just the right words. Simple sentences—*the theme is the lesson about life that the author wants us to ponder*—can be used over and over to help students remember, understand, and internalize sophisticated ideas. That said, you shouldn't read a lesson verbatim. Use your planning sheet as you would a list of talking points, and once you have found just the right words, you will own them.

Guided Practice

Evaluate the sophistication of what you are asking the students to do and the level of support they will need as they attempt it on their own. Sometimes they will first need to practice together as a group, then with a partner. Other times they may first need the safety of sharing their thinking with a partner before working as a class. Only you know your students and the level of support they need. And only you are with your class as the lesson unfolds. Use the appropriate teaching moves to scaffold your instruction as needed.

Send-Off and Independent Practice

Be realistic. Independent practice is a natural extension of the lesson; ask nothing different from what your students have been doing with you. Remind them to keep doing what they have been practicing, using either the books they are reading on their own or the text you have provided. When students have lots of questions or don't accomplish what you've asked them to do, your send-off was probably presented improperly or conveyed unrealistic expectations.

Group Wrap-Up

This is the moment for reflection. Wrap up the conversation about the text, or help students pin down the literacy strategy they've learned. Lead a discussion, ask a few students to share their ideas with the class, or have partners share with one another. The goal is for students to realize that this strategy is another tool they can use to become stronger readers, thinkers, speakers, and writers.

Don't Be Afraid to Revise

Knowing that you ask your students to take risks every day should inspire you to do the same. When the unit is finished, give it a try. It's a draft of your best thinking at that particular time. Finding the right words for each lesson can be a challenge. As you present the lessons, observe your fourth graders' responses and look for evidence that they understand. Repeat the lessons if necessary. Revise them based on your expertise, your knowledge of children, and your ability to be responsive to each learner. Find your own teaching voice and keep students at the center of your teaching.

Appendices

Appendix A
Initial Reading Conference Form

Student ______________________________ Date________________

Grade ________________

Teacher Question/Request	Student Response	Resulting Goals for Instruction
What book are you reading?		
How do you select books for independent reading? What do you look for?		
Why did you pick this book?		
What is your favorite kind of book to read? Why?		
What is happening in the story?		
Read a bit aloud to me. *While the child is reading, make the following determinations.* *Is it a just-right book?* *List any decoding errors.* *Comment on fluency.* *List evidence of comprehension.* *Can the student discuss the text fluently?* *At a point, stop and ask,* What are you thinking?		
What do you do if you find what you're reading confusing?		
What do you do if you come to a word you don't know?		
What is a goal you have for yourself as a reader?		

Observations:

Appendix B
Conference Sheet

Date/Text	Notes and Observations	Teaching Points and Goals

Appendix C
Synthesis Grid for Author Study

Author ______________________

Title	Characters	Setting	Plot	Illustrations	Theme	Craft (Ways with Words/Structures)	Other Noticings

Appendix D
Internet Research Grid for Author Study

Reference Source	Books	Awards/Medals	Biographical Information	How Person Became and Author	Other Interesting Information

Appendix E
Author's Craft

Title ____

Author ____

Genre ____

Notice	Example	Why did the author do this?
Ways with Words:		
Ways with Structure:		

Appendix F
120 High-Frequency Words

a	girl	night	then
about	go	no	there
after	good	not	these
all	had	now	they
an	has	of	they're
and	have	off	this
are	he	on	thought
as	her	one	through
at	him	or	time
be	his	other	to
because	home	our	too
before	how	out	two
but	I	over	up
by	if	people	very
can	in	play	want
can't	into	pretty	was
come	is	right	we
could	it	said	went
did	its	school	were
do	know	see	what
does	like	she	when
don't	little	so	where
down	made	some	which
each	make	talk	who
favorite	many	teacher	will
first	more	than	with
for	most	that	would
friend	much	the	write
from	my	their	you
get	new	them	your

Appendix G
Recommended Professional Resources

Nonfiction

Fountas, Irene, and Gay Su Pinnell. 2006. *Teaching for Comprehending and Fluency: Thinking, Talking, and Writing About Reading, K–8*. Portsmouth, NH: Heinemann.

Harvey, Stephanie. 1998. *Nonfiction Matters*. York, ME: Stenhouse.

Harvey, Stephanie, and Anne Goudvis. 2005. *The Comprehension Toolkit: Language and Lessons for Active Literacy*. Portsmouth, NH: Heinemann.

———. 2007. *Strategies That Work: Teaching Comprehension for Understanding and Engagement*. 2d ed. Portland, ME: Stenhouse.

Kristo, Janice, and Rosemary Bamford. 2004. *Nonfiction in Focus: A Comprehensive Framework for Helping Students Become Independent Readers and Writers of Nonfiction, K–6*. New York: Scholastic.

Interactive Read-Aloud

Calkins, Lucy M. 2001. "A Curriculum of Talk." In *The Art of Teaching Reading*, 225–47. Boston: Allyn and Bacon.

Cole, Ardith Davis. 2003. *Knee to Knee, Eye to Eye: Circling in on Comprehension*. Portsmouth, NH: Heinemann.

Fountas, Irene, and Gay Su Pinnell. 2006. *Teaching for Comprehending and Fluency: Thinking, Talking, and Writing About Reading*, K–8. Portsmouth, NH: Heinemann.

Nichols, Maria. 2006. *Comprehension Through Conversation: The Power of Purposeful Talk in the Reading Workshop*. Portsmouth, NH: Heinemann.

Appendix H
Suggested Collections of Short Texts

Dahl, Roald. 2000. *It's Great to Be Eight*. New York: Scholastic.

Erlich, Amy. 1996. *When I Was Your Age: Stories About Growing Up*. Vol. I. Cambridge, MA: Candlewick.

Greenfield, Eloise, and Lessie Jones Little. 1979. *Childtimes: A Three Generation Memoir*. New York: HarperCollins.

Graves, Donald. 1996. *Baseball, Snakes, and Summer Squash*. Honesdale, PA: Boyds Mills.

Jimenez, Francisco. 1997. *The Circuit*. New York: Houghton Mifflin.

Little, Jean. 1986. *Hey World, Here I Am*. New York: HarperTrophy.

Rylant, Cynthia. 1985. *Every Living Thing*. New York: Aladdin.

Scieszka, Jon, ed. 2005. *Guys Write for Guys Read*. New York: Viking.

Appendix I
Suggested Chapter Books for Interactive Read-Aloud Discussions

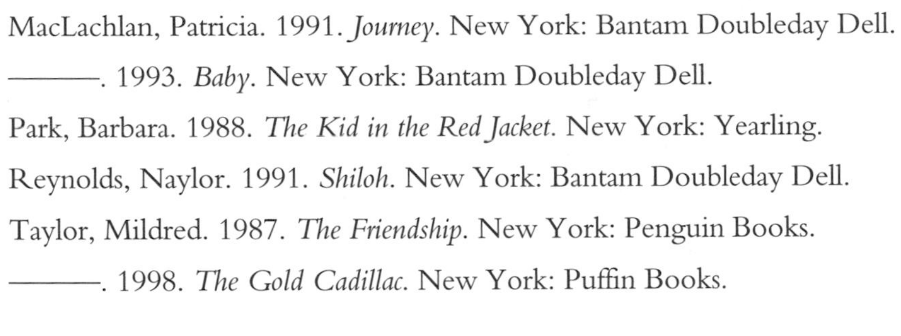

MacLachlan, Patricia. 1991. *Journey*. New York: Bantam Doubleday Dell.

———. 1993. *Baby*. New York: Bantam Doubleday Dell.

Park, Barbara. 1988. *The Kid in the Red Jacket*. New York: Yearling.

Reynolds, Naylor. 1991. *Shiloh*. New York: Bantam Doubleday Dell.

Taylor, Mildred. 1987. *The Friendship*. New York: Penguin Books.

———. 1998. *The Gold Cadillac*. New York: Puffin Books.

Appendix J
Thinkmark Templates

Thinkmark Record thinking, theories, reactions, confusions, wonderings, etc.
Pg.
Pg.
Pg.
Pg.
Possible Big Idea(s)

Thinkmark Record thinking, theories, reactions, confusions, wonderings, etc.
Pg.
Pg.
Pg.
Pg.
Possible Big Idea(s)

Appendix K
Learning About the Character

Name ______________________________

Title ______________________________

Character ______________________________

	Page # and Evidence	Page # and Evidence	Page # and Evidence	Page # and Evidence
Looks				
Feels/Thinks				
Talks				
Behaves				
How Others Respond				

Appendix L
People Who Influenced the Subject of My Biography

Name ______________________________ Date ______________

Title ____

Subject of Biography ______________________________________

Name and Relationship of Person	How He or She Influenced the Subject	My Thinking

Appendix M
Mapping Units of Study for Grade 4

Month	Unit of Study	Focus Lesson Topic(s)
September		
October		
November		
December		
January		
February		
March		
April		
May–June		

Appendix N
Monthlong Focus Lesson Trajectory

Lesson	Lesson	Lesson	Lesson
Lesson	Lesson	Lesson	Lesson
Lesson	Lesson	Lesson	Lesson
Lesson	Lesson	Lesson	Lesson

Appendix O
Focus Lesson Planning Sheet 1 (Guided Practice)

Topic	
Special Notes	
Thinking Behind the Lesson	
Materials	
Connection	
Explicit Instruction	
Guided Practice	
Send-Off	
Group Wrap-Up	

Appendix P
Focus Lesson Planning Sheet 2 (Guided Interaction)

Topic	
Special Notes	
Thinking Behind the Lesson	
Materials	
Connection	
Explicit Instruction	
Guided Interaction	
Send-Off	
Group Wrap-Up	

Bibliography

Allen, Janet. 2000. *Yellow Brick Roads: Shared and Guided Paths to Independent Reading 4–12*. Portland, ME: Stenhouse.

Allington, Richard. 1995. *No Quick Fix: Rethinking Literacy Programs in America's Elementary Schools*. New York: Teachers College Press.

———. 2001. *What Really Matters for Struggling Readers: Designing Research-Based Programs*. New York: Addison Wesley Longman.

Angelillo, Janet. 2003. *Writing About Reading*. Portsmouth, NH: Heinemann.

Atwell, Nancie. 1998. *In the Middle*. Portsmouth, NH: Heinemann.

Beck, Isabel L., Margaret G. McKeown, and Linda Kucan. 2002. *Bringing Words to Life: Robust Vocabulary Instruction*. New York: Guildford.

Calkins, Lucy M. 2001. *The Art of Teaching Reading*. Boston: Allyn and Bacon.

Chall, Jean S. 1983. *Stages of Reading Development*. New York: McGraw-Hill.

Chambers, Aidan. 1996. *Tell Me: Children, Reading and Talk*. York, ME: Stenhouse.

Choice Literacy. www.choiceliteracy.com

Clay, Marie M. 2002. *An Observation Survey of Early Literacy Achievement*. 2d ed. Portsmouth, NH: Heinemann.

Cole, Ardith Davis. 2003. *Knee to Knee, Eye to Eye: Circling in on Comprehension*. Portsmouth, NH: Heinemann.

Collins, Kathy. 2004. *Growing Readers: Units of Study in the Primary Classroom*. Portland, ME: Stenhouse.

Dowhower, S. L. 1987. "Effects of Repeated Reading on Second Grade Transitional Readers' Fluency and Comprehension." *Reading Research Quarterly* 22: 389–406.

Duffy, Gerald. 2002. "The Case for Direct Explanation of Strategies." In *Comprehension Instruction: Research-Based Best Practices*. New York: Guilford.

———. 2003. *Explaining Reading: A Resource for Teaching Concepts, Skills, and Strategies*. New York: Guilford.

Fountas, Irene, and Gay Su Pinnell. 1999. *Matching Books to Readers*. Portsmouth, NH: Heinemann.

———. 2006. *Teaching for Comprehending and Fluency: Thinking, Talking, and Writing About Reading, K–8*. Portsmouth, NH: Heinemann.

Graves, Donald. 1989. *Investigate Nonfiction*. Portsmouth, NH: Heinemann.

———. 1991. *Build a Literate Classroom*. Portsmouth, NH: Heinemann.

———. 1998. *Nonfiction Matters*. York, ME: Stenhouse.

Harvey, Stephanie, and Anne Goudvis. 2005. *The Comprehension Toolkit: Language and Lessons for Active Literacy*. Portsmouth, NH: Heinemann.

———. 2007. *Strategies That Work: Teaching Comprehension for Understanding and Engagement*. 2d ed. Portland, ME: Stenhouse.

Keene, Ellin, and Susan Zimmermann. 2007. *Mosaic of Thought: Teaching Comprehension in a Reader's Workshop*. 2d ed. Portsmouth, NH: Heinemann.

Kristo, Janice, and Rosemary Bamford. 2004. *Nonfiction in Focus: A Comprehensive Framework for Helping Students Become Independent Readers and Writers of Nonfiction, K–6*. New York: Scholastic.

Lattimer, Heather. 2003. *Thinking Through Genre: Units of Study in Reading and Writing Workshops 4–12*. Portland, ME: Stenhouse.

Miller, Debbie. 2002. *Reading with Meaning: Teaching Comprehension in the Primary Grades*. Portland, ME: Stenhouse.

Nagy, William E., and Richard C. Anderson. 1984. "How Many Words Are There in Printed School English?" *Reading Research Quarterly* 19: 304–30.

Nia, Isoke. 1999. "Units of Study in the Writing Workshop." *Primary Voices K–6*, 8 (1), August. Urbana, IL: NCTE.

Nichols, Maria. 2006. *Comprehension Through Conversation: The Power of Purposeful Talk in the Reading Workshop*. Portsmouth, NH: Heinemann.

Pearson, P. David, J. A. Dole, G. G. Duffy, and L. R. Roehler. 1992. "Developing Expertise in Reading Comprehension: What Should Be Taught and How Should It Be Taught?" In *What Research Has to Say to the Teacher of Reading*, ed. J. Farstrup and S. Jay Samuels, 2d ed. Newark, DE: International Reading Association.

Pressley, Michael. 1976. "Mental Imagery Helps Eight-Year-Olds Remember What They Read." *Journal of Educational Psychology* 68: 355–59.

———. 2005. *Reading Instruction That Works: The Case for Balanced Teaching*. 3d ed. New York: Guilford.

Rasinski, Timothy. 2003. *The Fluent Reader.* New York: Scholastic.

Rasinski, Timothy, and Michael Opitz. 1998. *Good-Bye Round Robin.* Portsmouth, NH: Heinemann.

Ray, Katie Wood. 1999. *Wondrous Words: Writers and Writing in the Elementary Classroom.* Urbana, IL: National Council Teachers of English.

Routman, Regie. 2003. *Reading Essentials: The Specifics You Need to Teach Reading Well.* Portsmouth, NH: Heinemann.

Samuels, S. Jay. 1979. "The Method of Repeated Readings." *The Reading Teacher* 32: 403–8.

Szymusiak, Karen, and Franki Sibberson. 2001. *Beyond Leveled Books: Supporting Transitional Readers in Grades 2–5.* Portland, ME: Stenhouse.

Tomlinson, Carol Ann. 1995. *How to Differentiate Instruction in Mixed-Ability Classrooms.* Alexandria, VA: Association for Supervision and Curriculum Development.

Tomlinson, Carol Ann, and Caroline Cunningham Eidson. 2003. *Differentiation in Practice: A Resource Guide for Differentiating Curriculum, Grades K–5.* Alexandria, VA: Association for Supervision and Curriculum Development.